This is one of the most practical and refreshing books I've read in years. I always look forward to the next Erwin Lutzer book because I know I will grow from it. This one is no exception, and at the end of it lies freedom.

How to Break a Stubborn Habit will give you hope even if you've struggled for years with a stubborn behavior. You don't have to just roll over and accept your failures and defeats. This little book can be a God-sent lifeline in your tussles with temptation.

There are no banal platitudes here; no shallow quick fixes lie on these pages. This is the kind of truth Jesus spoke of that sets people free.

Skip Heitzig
Author and Pastor
Calvary Albuquerque

HOW TO BREAK
A STUBBORN
HABIT

ERWIN W. LUTZER

HARVEST HOUSE PUBLISHERS
EUGENE, OREGON

HOW TO BREAK A STUBBORN HABIT

Copyright © 2017 by Erwin W. Lutzer
Published by Harvest House Publishers
Eugene, Oregon 97402
www.harvesthousepublishers.com

ISBN 978-0-7369-7013-6 (pbk.)
ISBN 978-0-7369-7119-5 (eBook)

Library of Congress Cataloging-in-Publication Data
Names: Lutzer, Erwin W., author.
Title: How to break a stubborn habit / Erwin W. Lutzer.
Other titles: Getting to no
Description: Eugene, Oregon : Harvest House Publishers, 2017. | Originally
    published under title: Getting to no : how to break a stubborn habit :
    Colorado Springs, Colo. : David C Cook, 2007. | Includes bibliographical
    references.
Identifiers: LCCN 2017004435| ISBN 9780736970136 (pbk.) | ISBN 9780736971195
    (ebook)
Subjects: LCSH: Habit breaking—Religious aspects—Christianity. | Change
    (Psychology)—Religious aspects—Christianity.
Classification: LCC BV4598.7 .L88 2017 | DDC 248.4—dc23 LC record available at https://lccn
.loc.gov/2017004435

Printed in the United States of America

17 18 19 20 21 22 23 24 25 / BP-CD / 10 9 8 7 6 5 4 3 2 1

To all those who seek to have a passion for God
that is greater than their passion to live with a stubborn habit—
"You make known to me the path of life;
you will fill me with joy in your presence,
with eternal pleasures at your right hand" (Psalm 16:11).

CONTENTS

Foreword by Stephen Arterburn

When Dr. Lutzer asked me to write the foreword for this amazing book, I was deeply humbled and excited to do so. You see, Erwin is one of the most respected hearts and minds in my world of books and radios. He is read, heard, and quoted by thousands of pastors who respect him as much or more than I do. But more than that, I am honored to provide the opening for any book that can help people find their way out of a tough habit or two or three, which is exactly what this book does.

Beware of what you are about to undertake, though, because it will not be easy. Most of the time, one sorry habit does not stand alone. It keeps company with other destructive behaviors that are designed for only one thing: to destroy our ability to feel good about ourselves, those who love us, and the God who created us.

Sure, there was a time when such things used to feel good to us. Why, isn't that the reason God gave us the freedom of choice in the first place? So we could do what we want, when we want to? Well, perhaps not. Proverbs 14:12 tells us: "There is a way that appears to be right, but in the end it leads to death."

You see, life has many roads. Some of them seem wide and pleasant (the paths of least resistance), while others look hard and toilsome at first glance. And as we struggle with our various hurts, it just seems so right to take the easier way. But what few people will tell you is that once you are on this road, it can be very difficult to get off. Haven't you ever noticed how the expressway has fewer exits? Missing your exit may not seem like such a big deal at the time, but you soon realize you're in an unfamiliar place, miles away from your destination with no way to turn around.

At this point you must learn to make some difficult decisions. If you continue on your path (the expressway), the road will likely be smooth and straight. No one will bother you, and you can drive as fast as you like—at least until you run out of gas. But the farther you go, the more difficult it will be to find your way back. You may not know the side streets. There will be stoplights and stop signs and detours. Traveling down here can be slow, and it can be hard, but God never said this would be easy, did He? Quite to the contrary, in fact— God tells us that change can be painful. First Peter 4:1 says, "Since Christ suffered in his body, arm yourselves also with the same attitude, because whoever suffers in the body is done with sin."

That doesn't sound like very much fun, does it? You probably thought things would get easier when you finally decided to turn around. Well, be encouraged, because I actually think this is good news. Pain, you see, is a sign of progress. If you've ever experienced frostbite before, you know that the thawing process does not feel good. But pain, difficult though it may be, is a sign that the parts of you that were previously cut off are coming back to life. It's not easy to turn away from the pictures on your computer when you know no one is looking, and it doesn't feel good to curb your spending in order to pay off that debt. But such feelings are a sign that you've finally found the right path.

And what's more, we are not called to do this alone. Others have been here before, and can offer strength and guidance for the journey. We need those who care about us to help us do what we are not able to do ourselves. And that is where this book comes in.

It is my hope that through reading this book, you will not simply learn what it means to defeat a habit, but you will learn what it means to join in fellowship with your fellow brothers and sisters under a common goal—to experience the power and love of God and the freedom that He designed for us. So welcome to a journey that will not be pain-free, but one that will also be full of joy and victory. Believe me—it is certainly worth the wait.

—*Stephen Arterburn*

A Hand from Heaven

The philosopher Seneca cried, "Oh that a hand would come down from heaven and deliver me from my besetting sin!" His plea has been echoed throughout the centuries. We've all wished for the same miracle.

Stubborn habits begin innocently enough, but because we don't master them, they quickly master us. We all experience the cycle: enjoy a forbidden pleasure, feel guilty, determine never to do it again, take pride in brief moments of self-control, then fail once more. Each time we repeat the pattern the ruts are cut a bit deeper, the chain is pulled a bit tighter.

Excusing our behavior because "we're just human," we become pessimistic, even defiant, and soon find ourselves victimized by sinfulness that refuses to budge. This behavior pattern becomes so familiar that eventually we don't even want to change. As we settle into an uneasy smugness, we come to feel at home with our anger, lust, worry, eating habits, laziness, bitterness, and selfishness—except during our small and occasional attempts at correction. We may even begin to congratulate ourselves for these small bits of effort, though they result in no real, lasting transformation.

Can we really be delivered from the one-step-forward, two-steps-back routine? At times I've thought the answer was no. Despite my sincere attempts at yielding myself to God, I've retained certain weaknesses (*sins* is a more honest word), which I've concluded I would simply have to live with. After all, *no one* is perfect!

But I knew my private failure was no credit to Jesus Christ, who won me to Himself by dying on the cross and offering me eternal life. Did He not promise that we could be *free*? Through many failures and a few victories I've discovered that the most persistent sin can be dislodged. We *can* be free from sins, even the ones safely tucked away in the crevices of our souls.

In ancient times, large cities did not exist with unending suburban sprawl as they do now. Rather, all the inhabitants of a city lived within the confines of a giant wall that served as protection from outside forces. Oftentimes during battle an enemy would concentrate its attack on the weakest point of the wall in an effort to bring it down. Enemies habitually exploited the same weakness—with startling success. Wouldn't it have made sense for the inhabitants of the city then to rebuild the defective fortification in preparation for the next assault? In much the same way, we repeatedly succumb to the same temptations without a constructive program for strengthening our defenses. We accept failure as a way of life, reasoning, "That's just the way I am."

God has a different plan—for which He has given us a message of deliverance and hope. True, there are no easy miracles. Our success is neither instant nor automatic. Slick and easy solutions lead to false expectations, which in turn spawn disappointment and unbelief. Applying biblical principles takes time and discipline. But steady progress is possible. Even long-established and sinful behavioral patterns can be replaced by wholesome attitudes and actions.

Seneca did not know that his wish had been granted, that God has come down from heaven to deliver us from our besetting sins. This book presents a step-by-step route to the freedom Christ Jesus has brought to us.

And if you haven't already done so, I would encourage you to find one or more people to travel this journey with you. You'll find there is no greater support than a fellow believer who has struggled or is struggling with the same issues, and who shares the same desire to live differently. The Scriptures tell us that "iron sharpens iron, so one person sharpens another" (Proverbs 27:17).

To this purpose, you'll find a series of questions at the end of each chapter. These are meant to help you digest what you read along the way—either as a group, with a partner, or individually. If you choose to go through this book with at least one other person, you'll also find the short discussion guide on pages 162-163 helpful.

In fact, you may find some of the principles helpful even if you work through this book on your own. Either way, I am excited to explore this path toward freedom with you, and I pray that you would be radically changed along the way.

Let me suggest that you read only one chapter of this book each day and think and act on what you have learned.

If you're ready...let's begin.

—Erwin W. Lutzer

CHAPTER 1

Why So Much Temptation?

As long as we are in our mortal bodies,
we will never outgrow temptation.

Why is lust so powerful?" Taylor asked. The weight of his guilt was crushing. He had fallen into sexual sin. "How can I trust myself? I don't want to live an immoral life. I promised myself I wouldn't do this, but here I am *again*."

A woman who for years had tried to quit smoking but always failed (regardless of the new remedy) once asked me, "Why is it that despite praying, yielding to God, and reading my Bible—why can't I quit no matter how hard I try?"

I have heard the same kind of questions from alcoholics and sex addicts who keep sliding back into the same destructive patterns of behavior no matter how many times they've dug themselves out.

Their questions deserve answers. Why is temptation so attractive, unrelenting, and powerful? Why doesn't God adjust the nature of our temptations so that the scales will be tipped more generously in our favor?

Whether it is trying to lose weight or struggling with alcohol or sexual addictions as habits, our temptations can be relentless. The Christian life does seem to be needlessly difficult at times. Surely God—the One who possesses all might and authority—could make it easier for those of us who love Him. So many believers succumb to one sin or another, often ending in ruin, so why doesn't God keep one step ahead of us, defusing the land mines along our path? If you are wondering how He could do so, consider these suggestions.

Satan Banned?

That's right—God could eliminate the devil. In fact, had He done that at the time of creation, chances are that Adam and Eve would not have plunged the human race into sin in the first place. Most likely, our first parents would have obeyed God without pausing to consider the fruit of the forbidden tree.

Assuming Adam and Eve held the same free will that we do now, why didn't God give them the opportunity to choose without outside interference? The serpent was beautiful, seemed to speak with authority, and promised a better life. As far as we know, Adam and Eve had not been told about the existence of Satan, and so were quite unprepared for this abrupt encounter. If the serpent had been barred from the Garden of Eden, Adam and Eve would have been more inclined to obey God. They might have chosen not to eat from the forbidden tree.

The presence of Satan in the garden, and his activity on our planet, tips the scales in favor of evil choices. I'm not saying we must follow his sinister suggestions, but if he were hidden away from our presence, we could resist temptation much more easily.

There's no doubt that much of the evil in the world, including our own struggles, can be traced to the interference of unseen spiritual forces. If God were to annihilate the devil, or at least confine him to the pit, we could take giant steps in our walk with the Lord. No more one-step-forward, two-steps-back routine! Our battle with temptation would be minimized, and we would be more inclined to resist the enticement of sin.

So why doesn't God just eliminate Satan?

Dampened Passions?

A second suggestion to minimize the daily failures of our Christian lives would be for God to dull the arrows of temptation that harass us from inside. James wrote, "Each person is tempted when they are dragged away by their own evil desire and enticed" (James 1:14). Could not God dampen those passions to bring moral purity more easily within reach? Surely He could help us feel just a bit less tempted—just enough so that we would be more likely to be victorious and a credit to our Redeemer.

We've all heard someone say, "I do not understand what I do. For what I want to do I do not do, but what I hate I do" (Romans 7:15). The church reformer John Knox wrote these words not long before he died:

> Now, after many battles, I find nothing in me but vanity and corruption. For in quietness I am negligent, in trouble impatient, tending to desperation; pride and ambition assault me on the one part, covetousness and malice trouble me on the other; briefly, O Lord, the affections of the flesh do almost suppress the operation of Thy Spirit.

If this man of God had such struggles, is there hope for the rest of us? God could make it easier for us, but He has chosen not to do so.

Rearranged Schedules?

Even if God did not banish the devil or dull our sinful passions, couldn't He guide us away from the places of temptation? Then we could be protected from circumstances that provoke us to sin.

David sinned with Bathsheba because she happened to be taking a bath next door while the king was resting on the rooftop. Couldn't that whole mess have been avoided if God had simply arranged for her to take her bath two hours earlier, or an hour later? Surely a sovereign God would have had no difficulty in rearranging the schedules of His finite creatures.

Didn't Achan sin because he saw a Babylonian garment left unattended after the siege of Jericho? Didn't Abraham lie because there was a famine in the land, and he feared for his life? Didn't Samson divulge the secret of his great strength because of his attraction to the charming Delilah?

Clearly God does not shield us from circumstances where we are vulnerable to sin. Remember, it was the Holy Spirit who led Jesus into the wilderness to be tempted of the devil. In the Lord's Prayer, Jesus taught His disciples to pray, "Lead us not into temptation, but deliver us from the evil one" (Matthew 6:13). We must admit that God does at times lead us into situations that stimulate our sinful desires, but this is not to say that God causes us to sin—nor does He tempt us in the same way as Satan. Rather, these are the times when we must lean on God and ask Him to save us, when we are otherwise incapable of saving ourselves.

James wrote, "When tempted, no one should say, 'God is tempting me.' For God cannot be tempted by evil, nor does he tempt anyone" (James 1:13). We cannot blame God for what we do. If we sin, it is because of our sinful nature; therefore we are responsible. But God does *test* us, and that testing often involves temptation. Quite unintentionally on our part, we sometimes find ourselves in situations that are an outward stimulus to sin.

Consider one married woman who, after running into a former boyfriend, discovered that she was still in love with him. Consequently, she began to think she had married the wrong man, and felt trapped. She began asking, "Why did God, who knows how weak I am, allow us to meet again?"

Or consider a person struggling with homosexual thoughts and behavior. She admitted that her abnormal desires had begun when, at the age of 12, she was forced into a sexual encounter with an older man. So began a long struggle with sexual temptation. Could not God have protected her from this experience?

Another person, trying desperately to break his smoking habit, said that he was making progress until he was transferred to an office where everyone smoked. In an atmosphere drenched with the smell of tobacco, he fell back into his former habit.

Alcoholics, trying to stay sober, often slip back into drunkenness because of pressure from friends who do not understand the depths of the alcoholic's weakness. So it goes.

And what about the more subtle sins of the mind? Yes, Jesus taught that evil originates in the heart, but many of our struggles with evil thoughts are provoked by our environment. Those of us who travel don't ask for a room that has ready access to pornography—but we get it anyway. But whether we travel or not, all around us are stimuli that draw out the worst in us. Without taking us out of the world, God could lead us into circumstances less conducive to evil passions, covetousness, and anger. If at least some of the potholes were removed from our paths, the possibility of blowouts would be lessened.

But God has not shielded us from the places or the power of cruel temptations. Satan has access to our lives (we will speak about this in detail later); our sin nature is unrestricted, and often without warning we find ourselves in situations that contribute to secret—or not so secret—sin.

Which brings us back to Taylor's original question: Why is temptation so powerful? Why is the struggle so intense?

Some Reasons for Temptation

A Test of Loyalty

As might be expected, God has a purpose in allowing us to be tempted. To begin, *let's remember that temptation, with all of its frightful possibilities for failure, is God's method of testing our loyalties.* We cannot say we love or trust someone until we have had to make some hard choices on that person's behalf. Similarly, we cannot say we love or trust God unless we have said no to persistent temptations. Quite simply, *God wants us to develop a passion for Him that is greater than our passion to sin!*

Take Abraham as an example. God asked him to slay his favorite son. He was strongly tempted to say no to God. The altar he built was probably the most carefully constructed altar ever made, as he probably took his time with it. As he worked, he surely thought of numerous reasons why he should disobey God—a key one being that Isaac was needed to fulfill God's promise of future generations of descendants. What is more, Sarah would never understand. And above all, how could a merciful God expect a man to slay his own beloved son?

Of course, you know how the story ended. Abraham passed the test; the angel of the Lord prevented him from stabbing his son and provided a ram for the sacrifice. Take note of God's perspective on the incident: "Now I know that you fear God, because you have not withheld from me your son, your only son" (Genesis 22:12). How do we know that Abraham loved God? That he trusted God?

Because he chose to say yes when all the powers of hell and the passions of his soul were crying no. This fierce temptation gave Abraham a striking opportunity to prove his love for the Almighty.

Let's return to some of those situations we mentioned earlier. What about the woman who seemingly could not resist falling in love with another man? Or the alcoholic tempted by his friends to revert to his old habits? Or the young man surrounded by the wrong crowd? Why does God not shield us from these circumstances? He allows us the luxury of difficult choices so that we can prove our love for Him. These are our opportunities to choose God rather than the world.

Do you love God?

I'm glad you said *yes.* But what happens when you are confronted with a tough decision—such as whether you should satisfy your passions or control them? Our response to temptation is an accurate barometer of our love for God. One of the first steps in handling temptation is to see it as an opportunity to test our loyalties. If we love the world, the love of the Father is not in us (1 John 2:15).

Joseph resisted the daily seduction of Potiphar's wife because of his love for God. He asked her, "How…could I do such a wicked thing and sin against God?" (Genesis 39:9). Even if he could have gotten by with his private affair without anyone finding out, he could not bear the thought of hurting the God he had come to know. The same principle applies to us. Each temptation leaves us better or worse; neutrality is impossible.

That's why God doesn't exterminate the devil and his demons.

Admittedly, the presence of wicked spirits in the world does make our choices more difficult. But think of what such agonizing choices mean to God. We prove our love for God when we say yes to Him, even when the deck appears to be stacked against us.

What it boils down to is this: Do we value the pleasures of the world, or those that come from God? The opportunities for sin that pop up around us, the sinful nature within us, and the demonic forces that influence us give us numerous opportunities to answer that question.

Transformed Passions

A second reason God does not make our choices easier is because *temptation is His vehicle for character development.* Sinful habits are a millstone about our necks, a weight on our souls. But that's only half the story!

These same temptations, struggles, and yes, even our sins are used by God to help us climb the ladder of spiritual maturity. If we see our sinful struggles only as a liability, we will never learn all that God wants to teach us through them.

There is a saying from Goethe, the German poet, that talent is formed in solitude, but character is developed in the storms of life. God wants to do something more beautiful in our lives than simply give us victory over a sin. He wants to replace it with something better—with the positive qualities of a fruitful life.

Temptation is God's magnifying glass; it shows us how much work He has left to do in our lives. When the Israelites were wandering in the wilderness, God let them become hungry and thirsty. On one occasion, they were even without water for three days. They became disappointed with their slow pace of travel; they were impatient with Moses' long rendezvous on Mount Sanai. Why didn't God meet their expectations? Listen to Moses' commentary: "Remember how the LORD your God led you all the way in the wilderness these forty years, to humble and test you in order to know what was in your heart, whether or not you would keep his commands" (Deuteronomy 8:2).

There it is again—God allowed the Israelites to suffer temptation to test their loyalties and to bring out their latent sinfulness. Temptation brings out the best or the worst in human beings. The Israelites didn't realize how rebellious they were until they got hungry. Temptation brings the impurities to the surface. Then God begins the siphoning process. Sometimes God teaches us these lessons by letting us suffer the consequences of our own sin. James wrote that we are enticed by our own lust. That word *entice* carries with it the imagery of a hunter who puts out bait for wild animals, or a housekeeper who sets a trap for a mouse. The mouse sees no valid reason why he should not eat that piece of cheese. Since his knowledge is limited, he cannot predict the future, and he doesn't understand traps. So he eats, and suffers a fatal outcome.

Some of us, thinking we can predict the consequences of our actions, assign a more serious result to overt sins than to those confined to thought and imagination. But even the secret sins, and of course addictions, exact their toll, and ultimately we can no longer control the sins—they control us. In time, God may dry up our fountains of pleasure and ambition so that we will turn to Him in repentance. But even then the battle is far from over.

God has given us the resources to do battle, and in the process He leads us to something better. He wants to develop within us the rich character qualities called the fruit of the Spirit: love, joy, and peace, to name a few (Galatians 5:22-23). God's purpose is to conform us to the image of His Son (Romans 8:29). To accomplish this goal, our character deficiencies (*sins* is a better word) must be brought to the surface so that we can be changed.

God also wants us to humble ourselves by seeking others for help and accountability. In the same way that a cut finger cannot be healed unless it is connected to the rest of the body, we cannot find relief from our sinful habits except through community with other believers. Secrecy and shame fuel addictions; only when we come to the light of God's presence and the openness of fellowship with others can we experience the kind of freedom we desire. Yes, we need the help of others. More on this subject later.

Temptation always involves risk-taking. The potential for devastating failure is ever present. But precisely because the stakes are so high, the rewards of resisting are so great. When we say no to temptation, we are saying yes to something far better.

Grace for Our Weakness

Finally, *God uses our sins to show us His grace and power on our behalf.* The depressing effect of sin is offset by the good news of God's grace. Paul wrote, "The law was brought in so that the trespass might increase. But where sin increased, grace increased all the more" (Romans 5:20).

Paul was given a thorn in the flesh so that he would remain humble. Perhaps it was a temptation he struggled to resist. He asked God three times for deliverance, but God said, "My grace is sufficient for you, for my power is made perfect in weakness" (2 Corinthians 12:9). Paul, therefore, boasted about his weakness, knowing that it provided an opportunity for God's power to rest upon him: "For when I am weak, then I am strong" (verse 10). If you are beset by an especially obstinate sin, you may be on the verge of seeing God's grace displayed in your life. Although you may now be preoccupied with your struggle, you may soon be preoccupied with your Savior.

God strikes at the core of our motivations. He is not interested in merely applying a new coat of paint, imposing a new set of rules. He wants to rebuild our minds and give us new values. The most important part of us is the part that nobody sees but God. And He wants to begin His work there.

Think about that one particular sin you struggle with most—the one that won't move off center stage in your life. Maybe it's an obvious one: drunkenness, overeating, drug addiction, or Internet pornography. Perhaps your imagination isn't suitable for certain audiences—or even any audience. Or maybe it's a sin of the spirit, such as pride, anxiety, fear, or bitterness. Whatever it is, God can deliver you from that sin. He can help you track it down and, with the help of the body of Christ, root it out and put you on a better path. Sin need not have dominion over you. You can be sure that God will never take from you anything that is good. Rather, when you are ready, He will remove the evil and replace it with something far better. *He will tear down your fortress so that He can build an altar in its place.*

Are you ready for such a transformation? The next chapter will help you answer that question.

> **ACTION STEP:** Present yourself to God and ask Him to give you the faith to believe that you can experience genuine change in your attitude and behavior.

Questions for Personal Reflection or Group Study

1. John 3:21 says, "Whoever lives by the truth comes into the light." Take inventory of your life: What is your most persistent temptation? Be honest. Why is it so difficult for you to say no to this temptation and yes to God? In what situations do you most often encounter this temptation? What do you hope to gain from conquering this troubling part of your life?

   Judging others / cynisism / critical
   Driving, being in the community

   I want to see good in everyone, live a life pleasing to God, love others - fulfill the Great commandment

2. Read the story of Jesus' temptation in the desert (Matthew 4:1-11). List all the reasons He might have found it easy to give in to Satan's suggestions. Speculate as to what the consequences of such acts would have been. Contrast His response with the way the Israelites acted when they were hungry (Exodus 16; Numbers 11). What can we learn from this contrast between the Son of Man and the children of Israel?

   1) He was tired
   2) He was hungry
   3) He was exhausted
   4) It could have been easy
   5) Instant power

3. Before you read the next chapter, spend some quiet time in prayer with your own particular temptations or sins in mind. Ask God for wisdom in the following areas:

   a. to help you properly identify the cause of your defeat, and

   b. to understand that you have been given the grace that is necessary to overcome this habit or persistent sin.

4. If you are reading this book alone, ask God to reveal one or two other people with whom you might be able to share your struggles, or even invite to join you in your journey through this book.

5. Take a few moments right now to thank God for the good things He is already doing in your life and for what He will do in the days ahead—in particular, how He will show His strength and grace at the point of your weakness.

CHAPTER 2

The Ground Rules

God can use our struggles for His glory.

There are many support groups for those who are struggling with addictions or behavioral issues. This book is intended to uncover the spiritual issues involved in our lives that we need to face in order to experience not just behavioral change, but a change of attitude and heart.

We are so desperate to change our behavior we'll try anything!

Recently, I read that a drug company has been trying to produce a pill to treat addicted gamblers. However, tests have revealed that compulsive gamblers who took the drug did no better in curbing their gaming habit than a control group that took placebos. As of this writing, no drug has been found to cure people from the impulse of gambling, or for that matter, from other impulses that similarly destroy lives.

But countless people can tell how God has changed their lives— though He always does it on His terms. Before you can take steps toward positive change, you *must* accept three basic conditions. If you have trouble accepting any one of these conditions, you will continue to struggle with your unwanted habit or addiction.

So what are these essentials?

Believe That God Is Good

First, *you must believe that God is good*. Because of the evils that exist in the world, the goodness of God is one of the most difficult doctrines to accept. Yet unless you wholeheartedly believe in it, you will be paralyzed in your Christian growth.

It is not surprising that Satan's first move in the Garden of Eden was to cause Eve to doubt the goodness of God. Here are his words: "You will certainly not die…For God knows that when you eat from [the tree] your eyes will be opened, and you will be like God, knowing good and evil" (Genesis 3:4-5). His point was, "God is restricting you because He doesn't want you to achieve your potential! You have the inherent right to be like Him, but He won't let you—He is selfish and doesn't have your best interests in mind."

Satan convinced Eve to believe that God wanted to restrain her from developing her potential—her godhood, if you will. Eve believed the lie.

Today, Satan uses similar strategies to dissatisfy us with God's will. Our anger at circumstances and our rebellion against God's commandments stem from our lack of confidence in God's goodness. The single girl seeking a mate asks, "How can God be good? If He were, He'd bring me the companionship of a husband. Doesn't He know how lonely I am?"

The playboy reasons, "Why should God restrict me from pleasure? When I'm hungry I eat; when I want pleasure I should be able to have sex. A God who cramps my lifestyle isn't good. If He were good, He'd have me find somebody who would really satisfy me."

The alcoholic complains, "If God were good, He'd give me a decent job. After all, wasn't it financial pressure that drove me to drink? Why doesn't God get me out of this mess? God is good? Good for *what*?"

I counseled a woman who needed to confess the sin of bitterness. Her response was, "If God loves me, why did He allow my parents to treat me like they did? A good God would never have allowed that to happen!" She couldn't forgive her parents because she couldn't forgive God for what she perceived to be His lack of protection. Instead, she chose to be victimized by her circumstances.

If you are a worrier, you also doubt God's goodness. You are afraid God will bring circumstances into your life that will be too much for you to handle.

If you are greedy and covetous, you doubt whether God is being fair by not providing you everything others have and enjoy. If you experience uncontrollable anger, you are rebelling against God's will for your life.

Look closely at that sin you don't want to give up. The root of your stubborn insistence is a basic doubt of God's goodness. You do not trust Him to do the best for you because *your way* is better than His.

Let's return to the story in the Garden of Eden. Notice how Satan focused on a restriction and used it to blind Eve to God's blessing. Yes, there was one tree she could not enjoy, but presumably there were hundreds she could. Did Satan point out the many trees she was permitted to eat from? Hardly. He focused on one negative, and Eve forgot about God's generosity and grace. So it is today. Satan will urge you to focus on one issue, one aggravation, one restriction. At that moment, he'll try to convince you that God's way is not best, but takes second place to what he can offer you…or what you can offer yourself.

So I must ask: Do you doubt God's goodness? Are you fully prepared to agree that His will is perfect and acceptable? If He did deliver you from sensual thoughts, would you feel cheated? If He denied you the pleasure of marriage, would you feel ripped off? If you gained victory over tobacco or alcohol, would you be resentful because you had been denied this chance to feel good?

Perhaps now you are beginning to understand why you cannot begin to break your sinful habit unless you believe in God's goodness. The reason is simple: If you doubt God's goodness, you will want to turn to God only when you are in a predicament, but keep your options open after things have returned to normal. You will be convinced that God wants to rob you rather than enrich you if He brings about permanent changes in you or your lifestyle.

I've discovered that the most frustrating problem in helping those who come to me for counsel is simply that most people do not really want to change. Of course, they are prepared to make minor adjustments—particularly if their behavior is getting them into trouble. But most of them are comfortable with their sin as long as it doesn't get out of hand. They would prefer to just manage their sin and have God's input into their lives be kept to a minimum.

What causes this lack of enthusiasm for getting rid of sin? We are afraid that some worthwhile pleasure will pass us by. We question whether God's way is indeed the best. If we doubt God's goodness, we will not only resist change but will also fear it. A young man I counseled simply could not give his future to God for fear that God might require him to drop out of medical school. He doubted whether God's will for him would be the best.

Countless Christians resist surrender to God, frightened of what God might require of them. He might lead them to the mission field, let them remain single, or require that they give up their love of money or their pursuit of sinful pleasures.

When you doubt God's goodness, you hug sins tightly to your bosom, afraid that God will rob you of your crutch, your pastime, your pleasure. Occasionally, you are stirred to give up your sins, but you soon find you want them back.

But is your way really better than God's? Was Satan the good guy in the Garden of Eden? And God the villain? Jesus put the matter straight: "The thief comes only to steal and kill and destroy; I have come that they may have life, and have it to the full" (John 10:10). To believe that your way is better than God's way is to take your place with Adam and Eve and believe Satan's lie. No matter how many pleasures Satan offers you, his ultimate intention is to ruin you. Your destruction is his highest priority.

On the positive side, if you accept the fact that God is good, two results will follow: First, you will realize that you can surrender to Him without reservations or fear of being cheated; second, you will thirst for change, understanding that the temporary watering holes of the world cannot compare to the everlasting springs of life that are in Christ.

So, are you prepared to yield yourself wholly to God without conditions, without reservations, and without a hidden agenda? No matter how attractive your sinful habit is, are you willing to let God teach you that His way is perfect? If so, you will be prepared to part with your sin, knowing that God will replace it with something better. You will have passed the first test as a candidate for radical change.

Own Your Behavior

What is the second essential truth you must accept? It is that as an adult, *you are fully responsible for your behavior and attitudes.* All of us are born with a propensity to avoid blame. Children display a remarkable ability to shift responsibility to others. As our children were growing up, my wife and I observed that they could spontaneously, creatively, almost ingeniously invent excuses for their misbehavior.

Because self-exposure is so painful, we become experts in self-protection, defending ourselves, tweaking the facts, and making ourselves look much better than we really are. This game of hiding ourselves from ourselves and the consequences of our actions is the result of being born with a sin nature, but it is inconsistent with what Christ requires of us as we are learning to walk with Him.

The blame game of hiding began in Eden. God asked Adam, "Have you eaten from the tree that I commanded you not to eat from?" (Genesis 3:11). The question was straightforward, and could have been answered in one word—*yes.* But Adam responded, "The woman you put here with me—she gave me some fruit from the tree, and I ate it" (verse 12). What Adam really said was, "It's Your fault—I'm stuck with this weak-willed woman You created."

Notice Adam's logic. God created the woman, the woman ate the fruit, and then gave it to him. He believed that if God had not created Eve, or if Eve had not disobeyed, he would not have sinned. Hence, he was not blameworthy. In accepting responsibility, Eve fared no better. "The serpent deceived me, and I ate" (verse 13). You may have heard the saying, "Adam blamed Eve; Eve blamed the serpent; and the serpent didn't have a leg to stand on." No one was responsible; it was God's fault.

But was it really? True, God created the tree, the woman, the man, and even Lucifer, who became the devil. God could have created a garden without this forbidden tree and could have barred the serpent from entry. Yes, a sovereign God could have done it all differently. But *Eve made a choice, and so did Adam.* Thus they had to bear the full responsibility of their choice. The serpent also got his due. Each made a choice, and each deserved blame. In the garden, the matter of human responsibility was settled forever: Each individual must take responsibility for his or her choices.

Someone is reported to have said of Robert Kennedy's assassin, "I do not blame him, but the society that produced him." Will Rogers once aptly remarked that there are two eras in American history—the passing of the buffalo, and the passing of the buck!

We cannot exaggerate about the harm that has come to individuals from the teaching of Sigmund Freud that those who misbehave are sick. We do not hold people responsible for catching the flu, getting the measles, or having cancer. We have hospitals, not prisons, for the physically sick, simply because they bear no moral blame for their illness. The reprehensible Freudian implication about misbehavior is clear: If people are not responsible for physical illness, why should they be held responsible for their addictive behavior? To say that a rapist, murderer, or thief is sick is to conclude that he should not be subject to punishment. After all, he simply caught a strange disease—he is the victim of forces beyond his control.

Recently, my wife and I watched a TV interview in which a doctor argued that the peculiarities of human behavior stem from the birth experience. If a baby is born in a noisy, bright, and seemingly unfriendly delivery room, the newborn will develop hostility in adult life. It follows, then, that no one should be blamed for hostility.

There are those who reason that if a teenager is in trouble, it's the parents' fault—they were too strict or too lenient. Or perhaps it was the teenager's environment—he or she was brought up in a wealthy home. Everyone knows that wealth spawns boredom, and boredom breeds crime. Conversely, the youngster is not responsible for inappropriate, self-destructive, or even criminal behavior if he or she came from a poor home—poverty drives people to drugs, sex, and crime.

Please understand that I know there are many instances in which the parents are indeed to blame for their child's wrong behavior. Homes in which there is abuse, addictions, or rejection adversely affect the children. But at some point a teenager must take responsibility for his or her attitudes and actions. We must be able to say that a person's past does not define who he is or how she acts.

The Bible says we are all born with a propensity to sin. We are by nature "children of wrath" (Ephesians 2:3 NKJV), and therefore when we are left without restraints, we follow our basest inclinations. It's not until we realize our inability and need that we seek the help of God.

Is it possible to break free from sexual addiction? Not if you keep blaming your environment or your genes for your actions. One man who did experience freedom from his long-standing behavioral patterns said, "For years I believed that I could never be free because I had an abusive home life, so I kept blaming my parents. But as I began to read the Scriptures, I began to believe God could change me. The first step in that direction was when I took full responsibility for my behavior. No excuses; no alibis."

When something is called sin, there is the possibility of deliverance—for Jesus came to call sinners to repentance. Alcoholics are known for their ability to avoid responsibility for their behavior. Their spouse, their boss, their friends, or their neighborhood is to blame. However, the Bible teaches that each person is responsible for their own actions. No one can make us promiscuous, or give us an ulcer. As I have said, the abuse and betrayal of others can introduce us to sinful behavioral patterns. But ultimately, especially when we become adults, we must take full responsibility for how we respond to our past and our circumstances. And even in those instances where we are propelled by passions seemingly beyond our control, we still do the choosing. So we can still choose God's path no matter how difficult the journey.

Of course, as I've already implied, we must be sensitive when speaking about these matters. Some people have suffered physical and emotional abuse, and therefore have reacted in sinful ways to cope with their pain. But we are all accountable—to family members, employers, society, church, and ultimately to God. As a mature person, each of us needs to stop blaming and begin taking full responsibility for our reactions to our past, no matter how traumatic it might have been.

When we stop hiding and assume responsibility for our sin, we'll find that we are candidates for God's mercy and power. A friend of mine put it this way: "God occasionally cures illness, but He has a sure cure for sin." Assuming responsibility also restores our God-given dignity. God did not create us as victims of circumstance, nor even as slaves to our genetic makeup. Whatever circumstances our pasts may hold, we can rise above them into a future shaped by God's grace.

Like Adam, who tried to avoid responsibility for his sin by telling God, "The woman you put here with me...," we are all tempted to say, "The parents You gave me..." or "The friends You gave me..." or "The passions You gave me..." Many people have spent small fortunes on professional counseling when they could have solved their problems had they been willing to accept responsibility for their anger toward others and then subjected themselves to God's program for change as found in the Bible.

If we resist honest exposure, we will not be changed by the biblical truths that are intended to change us. The love and acceptance of God provides for us a safe place where we no longer need to pretend and impress others. Because we are loved, we can be honest with who we are; because we are accepted, we can let God change us with the sure knowledge that we stand in desperate need of His help. The hiding has to end, and the fear of the truth has to be faced in the presence of a loving and caring God.

If you are still struggling, and perhaps thinking that I don't understand how badly you were mistreated or why your particular situation is unique, then you have probably failed the second test and are not yet looking for God to help you make changes in your life. Only the person who says, "*I* have sinned" reaches out to receive God's mercy and grace.

It is resentment toward others and God that keeps us from taking full responsibility for our stubborn habits. We are angry with those who have adversely affected us, and we have hostility toward God because we have concluded that He bears ultimate responsibility for whatever happens in His world.

Trust in God's Grace

Someone has well said that the last addiction is the idea that we can fight our behavioral patterns alone, just by sheer willpower. So we promise ourselves that yes, we will not repeat our mistakes, but of course we do. That is why we desperately need to understand that our hope lies in the amazing grace of God.

Quite simply, *you must believe that deliverance is possible*. To Adam and Eve, who sinned so flagrantly, God made a promise that Satan's power would be crushed when He told the serpent, "I will put enmity between you and the woman, and between your offspring and hers; he will crush your head, and you will strike his heel" (Genesis 3:15). The message was clear: In the conflict, Satan would continue to cause trouble on this earth until God overcame him once and for all through Jesus, the offspring of the woman. And now because of what Jesus has done, victory over sin is a possibility for every person who trusts in Him for salvation and deliverance.

The New Testament is, above all else, a book of hope. It details how God fulfilled this promise of victory. There is no sin—no, not one—that must, out of necessity, crush you. God has dramatically provided a way of escape: "No temptation has overtaken you except what is common to mankind. And God is faithful; he will not let you be tempted beyond what you can bear. But when you are tempted, he will also provide a way out so that you can endure it" (1 Corinthians 10:13). In that verse, we notice two facts.

First, you cannot plead that your case is unique or special. True, no two situations are identical, but your basic struggles against the passions of the world, your sinful nature, and Satan are the same as what others have faced. You can take comfort in the fact that you are experiencing a temptation that someone else has already dealt with successfully. In the Bible, Joseph did not succumb to lust; Moses conquered pride; Elijah overcame depression.

But what of people involved in the more stubborn sins of idolatry, adultery, homosexuality, drunkenness, or lying? The New Testament church at Corinth had these kinds of people—people who had been freed from their sin. In his letter to them, Paul listed the above sins and then added, "That is what some of you were. But you were washed, you were sanctified, you were justified in the name of the Lord Jesus Christ and by the Spirit of our God" (1 Corinthians 6:11). Take hope in the thought that someone else has already faced and overcome your particular problem.

Second, Paul asserted that God would give you the resources to cope with temptation. A faithful God does not expect you to do what you cannot; He supplies the needed strength. Do you remember the story of the battle between the children of Israel and the Amalekites? When it was time for the battle, Moses said,

> "Tomorrow I will stand on top of the hill with the staff of God in my hands." So Joshua fought the Amalekites as Moses had ordered, and Moses, Aaron and Hur went to the top of the hill. As long as Moses held up his hands, the Israelites were winning, but whenever he lowered his hands, the Amalekites were winning...Aaron and Hur held [Moses'] hands up...so that his hands remained steady till sunset. So Joshua overcame the Amalekite army with the sword (Exodus 17:9-13).

We can only live as we should if we have help from the people of God. We all need someone to hold up our weak arms, to help us walk a straight path, to comfort us, to give us strength, to pray for us. However, if you say, "I can't" and let it go at that, you are calling into question the integrity of God's character or the validity of your own faith.

Why is it so essential for you to believe that victory over your sin is possible? Because *no one can win a war he or she believes can't be won!* To go to battle believing in advance that there can be no permanent victory is to succumb to the enemy before the campaign even gets under way.

Christians have often conceded to the enemy by assuming that some sins cannot be dislodged. Such unbelief breeds pessimism, disobedience, and despair. The teaching of the New Testament is that "everything is possible for one who believes" (Mark 9:23).

Name your sin right now and say, "Thank You, God, that deliverance from it is possible!" God has had a vast amount of experience in delivering His people from temptation—even from *your* specific temptation. Peter wrote, "The Lord knows how to rescue the godly from trials and to hold the unrighteous for punishment on the day of judgment" (2 Peter 2:9).

Are you prepared to believe that God is good? Are you willing to take fully responsibility for your behavior? And do you believe that God's grace is able to help you? If so, then get ready, because God is about to perform a powerful work of transformation in your life.

ACTION STEP: We cannot expect transformation of our attitudes and behavior until the barrier of resentment/anger is removed. Go to God and stay there as long as you need to, confessing all of your resentments and anger to Him. Be specific: name people, circumstances, etc., and let it all spill out. This may take some time, but do it!

1. This chapter identifies three necessary conditions you must accept if you want to say no to temptation and mean it. They include the belief that God is good, the understanding that you must accept full responsibility for your behavior, and the belief that deliverance is possible. Where are you right now with these conditions? What, if anything, is holding you back from fully believing these truths? Read the following verses and meditate on their application to your life: Luke 1:37; John 8:32; and Hebrews 3:12. Seek prayer from others for your perseverance against sin.

2. No doubt David spent time finding excuses for his sin with Bathsheba. For example, unexpected circumstances led him to notice her just when her husband was out of town. Couldn't God have controlled those circumstances? But eventually, David came to realize the fault was entirely his own. He couldn't blame anyone else.

   Read David's prayer of repentance in Psalm 51 with these questions in mind: What evidence is there that David finally took full responsibility for what he had done? What evidence is there that David realized that his sin was first against God and only secondarily a sin against others?

Now read Romans 1:18-32. Trace the downward spiral of sin by asking, Why is this man responsible for his behavior?

3. What do you think is the most difficult behavioral problem to overcome? Why do you think we so often fail to tap God's resources for help?

4. Which people in the Bible successfully resisted your particular temptation? Why do you think they were successful? Are there any people in your life right now who have successfully resisted this same temptation? If so, how can you gain their support and encouragement in your struggles?

5. Take a few moments now and thank God for the areas of your life in which you are already experiencing victory. Ask Him to help you remember those victories in times when you struggle with other areas of sin.

And, above all, leave your resentments in God's presence!

CHAPTER 3

Putting Your Past Behind You

For of all sad words of tongue or pen,
the saddest are these: "It might have been."

—JOHN GREENLEAF WHITTIER

"It might have been" has a way of catching up with us. We all know how painful regret can be. Regardless of how sheltered or permissive our past, all of us have at least one thing we wish we had done differently. "If only I had listened to my parents," or "If only I had chosen different friends," or "If only I had not gone out with that person," and on and on.

You must deal with your past before you can experience freedom in the future. The sin that troubles you today sank its roots into your life yesterday. You can't break your sinful habits until you insist on a new beginning. Satan is particularly adept at using your past to ruin your future. His weapon is the illegitimate use of guilt feelings. Sins multiply in the soil of discouragement. One offense easily leads to another. You are caught in a vicious cycle until you realize that your past need not control your future.

God promises a new beginning.

When I attended grade school in Canada, we often played "Fox and Goose" on the fresh, clean snow in the schoolyard. After about 15 minutes of playing tag, the trails would become so messy that we would move to a clean area and stake out new paths in the glistening snow. Soon we would have to move again, and then again, always searching for a fresh beginning.

I observed something at that time that stayed with me. Whenever we blazed a new trail, all of us children were anxious to stay within its bounds. But after the trail became wide and untidy, we were less careful about spoiling the pattern in the snow. In fact, after about ten minutes of rowdy play we didn't care how the trails looked. We even deliberately made the playing area as messy as possible.

What a picture of humanity! I think of a young Christian woman who expressed a sincere desire to serve God. Her way of life was prudent, respectable, and moral. But then, contrary to her intentions, she succumbed to sexual sin. She felt overwhelmed with guilt and the realization that she could never recover her virginity. Thinking that a new beginning was impossible, she threw all caution to the wind and sought sexual excitement with different partners. When this woman became pregnant, she did not even know who had fathered the child.

So it is with many who become trapped in one sin or another. Sinful habits have a domino effect. The common feeling is, "If I do it once, I might as well go all the way and do it as often as I like." That's why some Christians question whether God can change them. They believe they cannot live differently in the future because of the past.

Satan delights in this kind of logic. He wants us to think that we have gone too far, that since the past cannot be reclaimed, we might as well give up. James Stalker, the Scottish preacher, wrote, "The great tempter of men has two lies with which he plies us at two different stages: Before we have fallen he tells us that one fall does not matter; it is a trifle; we can easily recover ourselves again. After we have fallen he tells us that it is hopeless; we are given over to sin, and need not attempt to rise." [1]

Stalker went to explain that both of these notions are false. *One fall does matter.* Even one fall can cause you to lose something that can never be recovered. An exquisite vessel can be broken and mended, but it will never be the same. Also, one sin leads to others. It's like climbing up an icy hill. Even as you attempt to rise, you fall again.

But when you do fall, you dare not accept Satan's second lie; namely, that there is no use in attempting to rise. Your enemy wants you to believe that since the past cannot be reclaimed, there is no way to break from its power.

Can you have a new beginning? In one sense, no, since the past cannot be relived. Virginity cannot be recovered; ruined health from nicotine, drugs, or gluttony may have to be accepted; a broken home may never be pieced back together. Even forgiven sin has its consequences. But in a deeply profound sense, you can have a new beginning. God offers two precious commodities: (1) genuine forgiveness, a blotting out of all your sins—past, present, and future; and (2) the assurance that your past need not control your future. The cycle of sin can be broken. You can rise again.

Listen to God's promise to an Israel possessed with violence, deceit, and sensual corruption: "Come now, let us settle the matter… Though your sins are like scarlet, they shall be as white as snow; though they are red as crimson, they shall be like wool" (Isaiah 1:18).

Although a messy "Fox and Goose" trail cannot be straightened out, a fresh blanket of snow can cover it. The spoiled paths, the soiled places in your life, can be covered by forgiveness. Your blood-red sins can become as white as snow. You too can have a new beginning.

The Consequences of Guilt

But to deal with the past, you must first deal with guilt. Feelings of guilt can be like a millstone around your neck, keeping you tied to your sins and wedded to your past failures. Sometimes your conscience may trouble you, rehearsing the sins of your past in vivid detail. Or you may sense a vague feeling of being under condemnation, a confirmed suspicion that you've blown it again. For that reason, you assume that you will always be a second-class citizen in the kingdom of heaven.

Living with guilt is like trying to drive a car with the brakes on.

Guilty feelings can produce many serious consequences:

Physical illness is often caused by suppressed guilt. Some doctors have estimated that nearly half of their patients could be released if they could be told with authority, "You are forgiven." Psychologists have said that the energy spent on keeping guilt out of one's mind can put a strain on the body and cause it to break down.

Unresolved guilt causes depression. Feelings of hopelessness and worthlessness are generated by the nagging feeling that you've blown it, and because the past cannot be reclaimed, there is little use trying to live a fruitful life.

√ Guilt is often the cause for lack of faith in God. First John 3:21 reads, "Dear friends, if our hearts do not condemn us, we have confidence before God." I've discovered in my counseling ministry that perhaps the most widespread cause of doubt is guilt. A person who feels impure will struggle with trust in God.

Guilt causes people to punish themselves. For example, some parents whose children have gone astray feel that they must punish themselves for what happened. They believe they must pay for their children's behavior, and that guilt is the price of the ticket. Others take this feeling a step further and interpret every tragedy as God's way of punishing them. Some people actually long to become physically sick so that they will have the satisfaction of "paying" for their sins. Yet such guilt feelings are never appeased, no matter how much a person suffers.

Guilt often causes people to do good works in an attempt to make up for past wrongdoing. A husband brings flowers to his wife in the evening because he shouted angrily at her in the morning. Some people give money to the church or are extra kind to a needy friend in the hope of atoning for their sins. Some children who have rebelled against their parents become burdened for social concerns and even work in impoverished communities to try to make amends for their rebellion. Rather than ask their parents' forgiveness, they assume that their sacrificial acts will help balance the books.

√ But good works never erase guilt. Good activity can suppress guilt, or help you to deny it, or buy time with your conscience. But the guilt will soon surface in another form. A friend of mine says that it's like spilling ketchup on your tie. Resolutions to be more careful next time, or even the determination to become a self-sacrificing slave, will never erase the stain. Until a remedy is found that can be applied directly to the guilt, it is there to stay. Fortunately, God has not left ✓ you without hope.

Principles for Handling Guilt

God's will is that you be free from all forms of guilt. He who is rich in mercy anticipated your moral and emotional entanglements. Fortunately, God is never taken by surprise. He offers you freedom from a nagging conscience. Let me suggest three steps toward finding this freedom.

First, identify the cause of your guilt feelings. This can often be done easily—an immoral relationship, cheating on your income tax, a harsh word to your parents—all these sources of guilt are quite easy to identify. Perhaps you will want to list these causes on a sheet of paper and then deal with each one specifically so you can put them behind you once and for all.

Let me warn you that sometimes people experience false guilt, bringing torment upon themselves for matters beyond their control. A woman and her three-year-old daughter stood at a curb, waiting to cross the street. The child asked, "Mother, can I go now?" Absent-mindedly, the mother answered, "Yes." Seconds later, she watched in horror as her three-year-old daughter was crushed to death by an oncoming truck. The horror of that event will never be erased from this woman's mind.

Afterward, she was plagued with guilt, a persistent feeling of regret, and self-loathing. She has since not been able to forgive herself. We can, of course, understand her remorse. But there must come a time when we put our debilitating feelings behind us, knowing that they come from within and not from God, who will not condemn us for accidents that occur outside our control. This woman needs to forgive herself and to realize that self-incrimination is not what God desires.

To overcome guilt feelings, bring them into the open, where you can deal with them. Ask yourself honestly why you are feeling guilty.

Second, realize that God's remedy for sin is complete. In Christ, God anticipated all of your feelings, discouragement, and failures. Jesus' death on the cross included a sacrifice for all our sins—past, present, and future. "When you were dead in your sins and in the uncircumcision of your flesh, God made you alive with Christ. He forgave us all our sins" (Colossians 2:13). Every sin you will ever commit has already been paid for. All your sins were future sins when Jesus died 2000 years ago. There is no sin that you will ever commit that has not *already* been included in Christ's death. Sins the devil reminds us of were included in the sacrifice of Christ. As Martin Luther said, "My sins are not mine but belong to Jesus."

God does not find it hard to forgive. It is not as though He regrets giving you a second chance. The price for forgiveness has already been paid, and God wants you to accept it freely.

Reportedly an atheist once asked Billy Graham something to this effect: "If Hitler had received Christ as Savior on his deathbed, would he have gone to heaven, and would someone who lived a good life but rejected Christ then go to hell?" This was a trick question. It was asked in such a way as to make the gospel appear ridiculous. But the answer is yes. If someone such as Hitler accepted Christ, God would forgive him completely, because Christ's death is sufficient for even the worst of sins. God values Christ so much that He would accept even Hitler under the merit of Christ, but He would not accept even the cleanest person without Christ, for no one is innocent apart from Him.

Jesus' cry from the cross—"It is finished" (John 19:30)—is but one word in the original Greek text, *tetelestai*. That word was used to refer to business transactions. When this word was written on a bill, it meant "paid in full." You need never try to make up for your sins on your own. Jesus' death paid for your sins *in full*.

When God forgives you, your sins are blotted out so completely that He does not remember them (Hebrews 8:12). He never holds them against you (Hebrews 10:17). The sins you confessed yesterday will never again be a barrier between you and God—unless you refuse to accept God's forgiveness or you doubt the value of Jesus' sacrifice.

I'm so glad my computer has a delete key. If I get my information wrong, or I need to rewrite a paragraph, I simply press the delete key, the past is gone, and I get the privilege of starting fresh. That's what happens to your sins when God forgives you. The consequences often remain, but the guilt, the legal condemnation for the offense, is gone.

I remember counseling a woman who was living with unresolved guilt from premarital sexual experiences. Her guilt and subsequent unhappy marriage had destroyed her health. I asked her if she had confessed her sins of the past. "Oh, yes, I've confessed those sins a thousand times," she replied. "Well, has God forgiven you?" I asked. Her answer was, "I'm not sure."

What was this woman really saying? She was denying that God had included her sin in Jesus' death. And she was also saying that God was not faithful to forgive us our sins and cleanse us from all unrighteousness as He promised (1 John 1:9).

Why do people constantly reconfess the same sins? Sometimes it's because they cannot believe that God would actually forgive so freely—surely they must suffer guilt first. Often they doubt whether they were sincere when they confessed their sins the first time. Or maybe they have never experienced grace and forgiveness from another person. Whatever the cause, as long as they feel guilty, Satan is winning a victory.

The Bible presents Satan as the accuser of the brethren. He brings their sins before them and before God during the night and during the day, but thankfully the redeemed can overcome him by the blood of the Lamb (Revelation 12:10-11).

Satan delights in having believers reconfess the same sins over and over. "Why don't you confess that sin again?" he suggests to our mind. The next day he tells us that we were insincere. "Confess that sin once more, but this time *really* mean business." And so it goes. If we fall for his deception, we are trapped by our own unbelief and become the victim of our own emotions. The result: no love, joy, or peace. We miserably sit on the shelf labeled "Unsure of Forgiveness"—a shelf already populated by scores of spiritually paralyzed saints.

And how do we distinguish between the promptings of the Holy Spirit and the accusations of the devil? The devil accuses us of sins that are already under the blood of Jesus—he accuses us of sins that God has already forgiven. The Holy Spirit convicts us of unconfessed sins that we must repent of so that fellowship with God is restored. But once we have repented and received forgiveness, the Holy Spirit has done His work.

How do you avoid this trap? The secret is to *thank God for your forgiveness even when you still feel guilty*. Use your guilt feelings as a reminder to give praise to God for His forgiveness. Memorize Psalms 32 and 103 and recite them with thanksgiving to God when those guilt feelings surface. This will become a great stepping-stone in your life, for you will learn to walk by faith, not by the whims of your emotions. And soon your feelings will catch up with your theology!

God promises you cleansing as well as forgiveness. Let's look at 1 John 1:9 more carefully: "If we confess our sins, He is faithful and just to forgive us our sins and to cleanse us from all unrighteousness" (NKJV). *Forgiveness* refers to what God has done objectively to restore us to fellowship, and *cleansing* is what God does to ensure that we know we've been forgiven. Or, to put it differently, cleansing is the subjective work of God whereby we are actually made clean.

A man struggling with Internet pornography once told me that even as he viewed the pictures, he confessed his sin—perhaps as often as two or three times a minute. But he discovered that, even after confession, his passions would continue. This is obvious proof that even confession in itself does not stop lustful desires once they are set in motion. But this man discovered the antidote to his problem. When he insisted not merely on God's forgiveness but also on God's cleansing, he knew he would have to turn off the computer. He said,

"Sometimes I could feel the lust leave my body when I determined to accept God's cleansing."

Of course this did not end his battle; God intends that we come to spiritual freedom in community—that is, by having others walk with us along the same path toward freedom and wholeness.

By receiving forgiveness and inner cleansing, you can take the first step in putting your past behind you. Much more must be done, but at least you have begun the process.

Accepting God's Grace

God's grace is greater than your sin, whether the offense is big or small. A well-known Christian, driving too fast in the rain, caused an accident in which his companion was killed. Regret and the pain of guilt erupted in this man's heart. Yet he decided that he would not spend the rest of his life in the prison of self-incrimination. He chose to forgive himself, knowing that God had forgiven him. "That night," he says, "I saw more clearly than ever before that the purpose of the cross is to repair the irreparable."

John Newton had godly parents but was orphaned at the age of six. He was adopted by a relative who rejected the boy's Christian heritage. At an early age, Newton became an apprentice seaman. While enlisted in the Royal Navy, he deserted and went to Africa for one purpose—to sin to his fill.

He became a servant to a wicked slave trader and began sinning beyond what even *he* was comfortable with! Eventually, he escaped to the coast. There he attracted a ship by building a signal fire. Because he was a skilled navigator, he was soon made a mate on the vessel, which was making its way up the coast of Africa to England.

On one occasion, he opened the casks of rum on board and distributed the liquor to the crew so that all the members became drunk. As the ship made its way to Great Britain, it was blown off course in a violent storm. When the ship began to flounder, Newton was sent into the hold to work the pumps along with the slaves who were being transported. At that moment the faith teachings he had received from his mother as a child came rushing back to him, and he cried out, "Lord, have mercy upon us!" The events that transpired on that day changed his life forever, and eventually he wrote those famous words:

> Amazing grace! How sweet the sound
> That saved a wretch like me!
> I once was lost, but now am found;
> Was blind, but now I see.[2]

If God is able to "forget" your past, why can't you? As one illustration puts it, when you confess your sins and ask forgiveness of them, God throws them into the depths of the sea, and then puts up a sign on the shore that reads, "No fishing."

Finally, pursue healing in all of your personal relationships. Many of us are in fellowship with God, but our consciences won't allow us to experience joy because we have unresolved matters between ourselves and others. These issues nag at our souls and remind us that not all is well in our delicately balanced psyches. Most of us, unfortunately, harden our hearts and simply choose to live with low-level guilt and inner irritations of conscience. Forgiveness and restitution—and whenever possible, restoration—is the only way to freedom. A telephone call or a casual meeting with a friend is often all that is needed to heal old wounds.

But what if the other person will not forgive you? If you have approached him or her in the right spirit, you can be confident that God's grace will work its way in time. But until then, be satisfied that you have done what you can to set wrongs right.

There is no reason for you to be trapped in the murky waters of your past. God offers you a new beginning. Jesus said to the woman taken in adultery, "Go, and sin no more" (John 8:11 KJV). Once your past is forgiven, you are free from its grip. You have been rescued from the waters of sin and now stand at a fork in the road. With your sins forgiven you can either return to the slippery slopes of failure or plant your feet on God's soil, standing firmly by His side.

ACTION STEP: Right now, if you haven't already done so, receive the gift of eternal life that Jesus Christ offers you. Then give your past to Him—the good, the bad, and the ugly. Ask Him to show you the steps you must take to connect with other believers, for change comes about in community. God will help you find a place to fit in.

Questions for Personal Reflection or Group Study

1. Psalm 32 is an account of how David felt when he tried to hide his sin. List the effects of unconfessed sin as mentioned in verses 3 through 5. Have you been feeling any of these effects lately? If so, what can you do to change that situation?

2. Think of various actions for which we often feel guilty because we cannot forgive ourselves. How can we know whether our guilt is brought about by ourselves or by God?

3. Reread the account of the fall of humanity in Genesis 3. What evidence is there that Adam and Eve felt guilty when God came to them? What characteristics of guilt are found in the record?

   What was God's response to Adam and Eve's need? In what ways can you relate to Adam and Eve's actions? How do you think God will respond to you when you come to Him with humility, seeking forgiveness?

4. Once we have confessed our sins, we must continually thank God for His pardon. Memorize these verses and recite them as an expression of praise to God for His forgiveness: Psalm 32:1-2; Romans 8:33-34; 1 John 1:9.

5. Take some time now to pray and think about the times when you have not felt forgiven for your sins. Ask God to change your attitude toward His sacrifice and to bring you to a place where you can accept His forgiveness and move forward. (Chapter 8 will further address how we separate our "feelings" from God's truth.)

CHAPTER 4

Seeing with God's Eyes

My problem is deep, but so is God's grace.

Are you still serious about breaking that sinful habit?

Good. Let's get started. Since it is essential that you see your problem in perspective, consider the following stories. Perhaps you can relate to one of them.

At a young age, Dave discovered that with the click of a button an entire world of Internet pornography was open to him. Years later, then married, he prayed to God for strength to overcome this addiction, earnestly pleading that his inappropriate sexual desires would diminish. He was submerged in guilt, fear, and shame because he couldn't resist the urge. Eventually his wife discovered the websites he had been viewing, and their relationship was deeply wounded.

Ken was a truck driver who promised his wife he would quit smoking. He decided to decrease the number of cigarettes he smoked each day until he was free from the habit. He failed so many times that he gave up. Today, he is convinced he can never quit and has no intention of trying.

Susan's first husband died young of a heart attack. Two years later she remarried. This time her husband was a Christian. After years of marriage to her new husband, though, she still longed for the intimacy she shared with her first husband. Ultimately she fell into an affair with another man. She prayed for hours at a time that God would release her from her desire to seek affection in unhealthy ways, but He never answered—at least not in a way that she could hear. Eventually the affair was discovered, and she and her new husband divorced.

John was a man with an explosive temper. Sharp words shot out of his mouth, shattering his wife's self-confidence and affection. He overdisciplined his children, usually in fits of anger. As a Christian, he knew better and even decided to change. Once, after a particularly sharp exchange with his wife, he put his fist through the wall. Humiliated and guilt-ridden, he asked God for deliverance from his temper. Vowing to change did not help; neither did praying. Months later he gave up, saying, "I can't help myself. That's just the way I am."

What went wrong? All of these people were Christians, all prayed to be delivered, yet all ended up more discouraged than when they began. The easy answer is to say, "They weren't sincere—if they had meant it, God would have helped them." However, many who are very sincere in their prayers—even to the point of genuine weeping—continue to struggle on a daily basis. Apparently sincerity in itself doesn't guarantee deliverance.

One reason people revert to their old behavior patterns is that *they misunderstand the full extent of their problem.* True, they want victory, but they don't understand how or why God will bring it about. Like them, most of us want to overcome a specific habit—for our own benefit. We want to be free of the symptoms of a problem, but avoid a thorough examination that might reveal deeper problems in our lives—problems that we are unwilling to face.

Habits themselves are like the tip of an iceberg, with 90 percent of the issue usually lying deeper under the surface. Let me explain: Dave wanted to break his pornography habit because he felt guilty; furthermore, he lived in constant fear of being discovered. He sought God's assistance to save his marriage and, above all, his reputation. This, of course, is understandable; we can all identify with such motivation. But his life needed many other adjustments.

First, he was selfish, spending much of his free time working on cars. He considered his family an inconvenience. How could he expect to defeat a sinful habit if he couldn't put others before himself? Second, he was prideful. Dave and his wife would often get into arguments, which he turned into opportunities to blame her for the circumstances in his life. He would rationalize that she didn't care about him enough—in fact, she was probably the reason this stubborn habit still persisted, though he knew well enough that this sin had been an issue long before he ever met her.

What was God's concern for this man? That he stop viewing pornography and lusting after women who were not his wife? Yes. But God wanted much more than that for Dave. God wanted him to humble himself, to ask the forgiveness of his wife and children, and to reorganize his priorities. Dave needed to connect with other Christian men who would be honest with him and hold him accountable. He had some bad attitudes he needed to confess, pride that he needed to break, and selfishness he needed to face head-on. More importantly, he needed to put God first in his life. But Dave wasn't concerned about such drastic treatment. God wanted to take charge of Dave's entire house, but Dave just wanted Him to sweep the front steps.

And what about Ken? He wanted to quit smoking. Yes, he was a Christian, but he lived only on the fringes of spiritual commitment. His children had never heard him pray except for the perfunctory grace said at mealtimes. He was not a spiritual leader in his home; his wife taught the children the few Bible stories they knew.

Now Ken wanted God to help him quit smoking because the doctors told him he might die of lung cancer. Could God help him overcome that habit? Yes indeed. But he would have to yield himself fully to God—his time, property, and reputation would have to be committed to the Almighty. Ken would have to begin reading the Scriptures and turning to God daily for his own needs and the needs of his family. But he didn't bargain for such changes. He thought God would deliver him from cigarettes and leave the rest of his life untouched.

And why didn't God deliver Susan from her perceived needs? Deep within, she faced long-standing struggles related to her first marriage that she had never resolved. She was also nervous and fearful, and had a history of nagging her husband and children about almost everything. Her present situation was inflamed with self-pity—one sin she was not prepared to part with. She continually justified her attitudes, extolling her own righteous behavior and bemoaning the fact that she, of all people, had been so sorely mistreated by the loss of her first husband.

We can sympathize with Susan. Her emotional anguish was enormous, even beyond description. But the fact remains that self-pity cannot be defeated until we take ownership of our behavior. For many people, even prayer itself becomes another self-pitying session in which God is informed—even blamed—in meticulous detail for all wrongs suffered.

Finally, there is John. He thought he was simply born with a short fuse. And of course, his circumstances were to blame—if everything would go more to his liking, there would be no need to blow up, no need to put his fist through the wall. But in reality, John was always angry—angry at his employer, angry at others, angry at life itself. He felt unworthy because he had not become the success his absentee father hoped for. John needed to face the feelings of rejection he suffered in his childhood and submit them to God for emotional healing—and he needed forgiveness to replace resentment.

John didn't realize it, but he was a man at war with God, rebelling against the vocation and the circumstances of life to which God had called him. Until he accepted himself and his place in the world with joyful thanksgiving, he would never learn to control his temper. God was concerned that John change his attitudes, but John wasn't willing. He wanted victory over his temper so he could avoid future embarrassment and keep his marriage intact. But all he wanted was the minimum required to keep his life on a fairly even keel—and no more.

Face the Issues

How easy it is to seek freedom from a particular sin without facing basic issues! One day, a man who had been fired from his job called me on the phone. I had never met him, but he asked me what he could do to develop his willpower. He simply could not get to work on time and had been fired from two previous jobs because of his laziness and lack of punctuality. I gave him some suggestions, hoping to help him.

A week later, I received a phone call from a woman seeking advice on how to end an illicit sexual affair. To my chagrin, the man she was involved with was the one I had spoken to a week earlier! His problem of sensuality had affected all areas of his life. How accurate James was when he taught that a double-minded man is unstable in *all* his ways (James 1:8). Sinful habits are usually indicative of unresolved conflicts. We must always look for underlying causes rather than just treat the symptoms. God uses our struggles with sin to diagnose our true condition. Temptation is His X-ray machine, revealing the hidden conflicts that need attention.

What Does God Want to Accomplish?

God has a larger purpose in wanting to show us our inner self. Unfortunately, we too often seek the lesser purpose: We desire freedom from sin to avoid embarrassment, to be relieved of guilt, or to save a marriage. However, the deeper issue we often avoid is our rebellion against God. A man may be dishonest in business; a woman may have had an abortion—both may want to be free from a nagging conscience, but they may not be willing to deal with their basic attitude of defiance toward God's authority.

Genuine repentance is never easy. To confess our sins means that we agree with God that we have sinned; it also means that we agree that the sin must be forsaken. Those who confess their sins yet intend to repeat the same action are only partially repentant—if at all. Such incomplete repentance leads to a downward spiral of repeated failure.

Confession means that we admit our sin and give God permission to remove it from our life. Of course, I'm not saying that we will *never* commit the same sin again—if so, none of us could claim forgiveness. But there needs to be a willingness to part with sin and a submission to God's verdict on the matter. Apart from such an acknowledgment, our intentions are self-centered. We are inquiring how forgiveness will benefit us instead of considering how we have offended God.

So, confess your sins to God and repent of them. But don't stop there. God wants to draw you beyond repentance to Himself. He wants to use your struggles to lead you into godly living. His will is not merely that you be free from sin; He wants to conform you to the image of His Son. Delivering you from sinful habits is only a step in the process. Washing the stains from your life is His prelude to changing you into the Spirit-filled person He wants you to be.

Sometimes those who were at one time the most hopeless end up being the most radically changed. The reason is because they are the most desperate when they finally come to the end of themselves. When they see themselves for what they really are, they will realize God's principles need to be applied to *all* areas of their life. Their struggles will drive them to become better acquainted with the Almighty and His Word. Their struggles will lead them toward God rather than away from Him.

When you are faced with excruciating temptation, you have a choice to make. You can say, "I've tried to change before, and it hasn't worked, so I'll manage the best I can with my sin. We're all human, you know." The result? Your sin will be a monument to the false god you have fashioned.

Or you can take a look at your sinful habit and see it as a challenge to display God's grace and power in your life. To the Jewish Christians scattered by persecution, James wrote, "Consider it pure joy, my brothers and sisters, whenever you face trials of many kinds, because you know that the testing of your faith produces perseverance. Let perseverance finish its work so that you may be mature and complete, not lacking anything" (James 1:2-4).

Our sin cost God the life of His Son; He is not about to hand out a spiritual Band-Aid to hide a spiritual cancer. God wants to use our struggles to help us see our need to do a thorough housecleaning, reorganize our priorities, and be fully dependent on His grace. There are no cheap, easy miracles. We must want spiritual freedom not merely for our own sake, but for God's sake as well. His glory is what really matters.

Getting a Larger Focus

Many Christians think that victory over sin means that they will no longer be tempted. Or they assume that God will change their nature so that they will no longer desire to do evil. Either way, they are wrong. Temptation in and of itself is not a sin; it is a call to battle.

Perhaps you have discovered, as I have, that God does not deliver us from temptation. He does not change our nature so that we are less than human. Temptation of one kind or another is universal. To pray that we will no longer be tempted is to ask that we die and go to heaven. Because we will always be tempted, we need to learn to handle temptation in God's way. Here are several steps to follow to ensure that you are dealing with temptation in a godly manner.

First, you must thank God for temptations and the opportunities they represent in your life. Each temptation gives you a clear-cut opportunity to declare your allegiance to Jesus Christ. Persistent praise is the first positive step toward overcoming temptation. God is glorified when you accept your circumstances as from His hand. If you cannot thank God for your condition and even your temptation, you are rebelling against Him. A man wrestling with a fierce temptation once told me he could not resist it until he gave thanks to God continually for his struggle. "Lord," he prayed, "I thank You for this temptation. Even if I should be tempted from now until the day I die, I give thanks for it."

This is the first step to handling temptation in a godly way. Accept the fact that you will be tempted; then choose to thank God for the opportunity it represents.

Second, spend some time defining your basic attitudes. Take a tour through your life and jot down the areas in which you need to do some work. What is it that *really* bothers you? What do you really want? Are you rebelling against some person? Are you upset with your performance? Your appearance? Do you feel like a failure? Do you think that you have been shortchanged since becoming a Christian? Are you bitter toward your parents, children, husband, or wife? Are you angry at God because He hasn't done what you think He ought? Spend at least an hour doing this personal inventory.

Whenever I do so, I always discover attitudes I didn't know I had. For example, I'm often upset with myself because it takes me so long to accomplish a project—writing a book, for instance. I'm preoccupied with struggles in the ministry, frustration in personal relationships, and responsibilities as a husband, father, and grandfather. All these things affect my attitude, my perspective. God has been showing me that the way I handle these attitudes will affect my relationship with Him and will bring either honor or dishonor to His name.

Third, after you have had time to reflect on your private struggles, give yourself and your problem completely to God. Give God the key to every room in your soul and let Him enter and take charge. Do so knowing that God will require you to deal with those attitudes and sins you have so carefully justified. This may be a long and painful process, but it can be lastingly beneficial.

Don't be afraid of what God might demand of you. A woman who was very shy and withdrawn once told me she was afraid to give herself to God because she might have to learn to be friendly. Undoubtedly you will face some difficult situations, especially those in which you will have to ask forgiveness of others. Some situations might even require the guidance of a biblical counselor. But I believe you will find that the pain is worth it as God works all things together for good in your life (Romans 8:28).

And whatever God asks of you, He will give you the strength to do. Perhaps you have come to a stream where the bridge has washed away—it still may be possible to cross the stream, though not in short steps. Now is the time for you to leap! So it is when you give yourself to God. When the bridge of blame and excuses is gone, take that one long jump without any thought of returning to a life of halfhearted commitment. Though your dedication may have to be renewed many times, make it as clear, specific, and final as you can, knowing God will be with you to keep you walking in His way.

Finally, realize that your ultimate goal is not victory, but relationship with God Himself. Augustine wrote in his *Confessions*, "O Lord, Thou hast made us for Thyself and our hearts are restless until they find their rest in Thee." Ultimately, not even victory over sin can satisfy our innermost desires. Only God can meet our deepest needs, for He has created us as social creatures, and we must be in relationship with Him to realize our full potential as His children. Hearts are changed the moment they accept Christ, but much more work is needed to change the thoughts and attitudes of the mind and the habits of the body.

Remember Copernicus? He was the astronomer who concluded that the earth rotated around the sun, and not vice versa. With the sun at the center of the universe, the planetary motion could be explained more easily. The complicated equations needed to explain the movement of the planets were simplified by this new theory.

God wants you to have your own Copernican revolution. He longs to be made the very center of your life—to reward you and bring your life meaning through serving the Sovereign who is both Creator and Redeemer. The victory over sin that you seek will come from your relationship with God. When you seek to know God and love Him with your whole mind, heart, and soul, the freedom you are looking for will become yours.

You may think that knowing God is a rather theoretical and mystical goal. God is invisible, and may seem inaccessible. Isn't it easier to establish goals in business or in your marriage and family life? The wonderful promise of the Scriptures is that you *can* know God. To the prophet Jeremiah God said, "You will seek me and find me when you seek me with all your heart. I will be found by you" (Jeremiah 29:13-14).

Throughout the Bible, the desire to know God is compared to a thirst. The Old Testament prophets spoke of the time when the land would be flowing with water, when God Himself would give His people springs in the desert. In the New Testament, Jesus spoke of Himself as the One who could provide living water. He said, "Let anyone who is thirsty come to me and drink. Whoever believes in me, as Scripture has said, rivers of living water will flow from within them" (John 7:37-38).

Are you thirsty for this living water, water that can satisfy the innermost reaches of your soul? Perhaps you can relate to these words from Nancy Spiegelberg: "Lord, I crawled across the barrenness to You with my empty cup, uncertain—but asking any small drop of refreshment. If only I had known you better I would have come running with a bucket."[3]

The better you know God, the more often you will turn to Him. The more you understand that you are created for fellowship with Him, the more time you will spend fulfilling that purpose until your life demonstrates the singleness of devotion that Paul expressed: "This one thing I do" (Philippians 3:13 KJV).

When you come to see yourself and your life from God's perspective, you will learn to pray optimistically and in faith. God has brought this temptation to you for your good. Now thank Him for how He will use it. He wants to build and not to destroy. If He wounds you, it is so that He might heal you in the depths of your being.

If you are serious about breaking that sinful habit, why not pray right now, thanking God for what He will do in your life?

ACTION STEP:

Father, give me the wisdom to see my struggles from Your point of view. I confess my cynicism because I feel so hopeless at times. Thank You for Your forgiveness. I am grateful for temptations, which give me the chance to prove that I love You more than any pleasure in the world. I thank You that the temptation is not greater than I can bear, and I rejoice at how You will use it in my life. I look forward to getting to know You better, and I am glad that You have sent me this trial as a reminder of how desperately I need You. Help me to remember to give thanks at all times and in all circumstances.

In Jesus' name. Amen.

Questions for Personal Reflection or Group Study

✓ 1. Most of our repeated failures stem from one of three basic causes: (a) pride, (b), sensuality, or (c) covetousness. Read Genesis 3:1-8 and try to find these three elements in Satan's temptation of Adam and Eve.

✓ 2. Try to relate your particular temptation to one or more of the root problems mentioned above. For example, the sin of anger actually reflects pride and an unwillingness to forgive those who have wronged us. Our expected struggles with lust are enflamed by pornography when we believe that these pleasures outweigh the benefits of obedience to God. What are some other examples you can think of?

✓ 3. Think of some Bible characters who tried to cover or excuse their sins. What was the result for them personally, and what was the result for the people around them?

4. In Galatians 5:19-21, Paul wrote a list of the works of the flesh. Review the list, and describe the way in which each sinful work is symptomatic of rebellion against God.

5. As you think about the particular sin you would like to overcome, ask yourself: What would God want me to put in the place of this habit? You may find it helpful to consider the character qualities God desires to build in your life, such as those listed in the Beatitudes (see Matthew 5:1-11) and those listed among the fruit of the Spirit (Galatians 5:22-23). Now spend some time in prayer and ask God to use your particular temptation as a catalyst that encourages you to cultivate positive character traits in your life.

CHAPTER 5

The Freedom of Living at the Cross

Jesus has already been where we need to go.

Let this statement bless your soul: *Everything God expects us to do is based on what He has already done for us.*

In other words, God anticipated our struggles, and in Jesus, our greatest spiritual need has been met. Thanks to Him, we do not have to be overwhelmed by our propensity to be caught in the vicious two-steps-forward-and-three-steps-back routine.

In this chapter we will review a bit of theology that will give us hope in our daily struggles. But first, let me give a further explanation of our dilemma.

When you try to break a sinful habit or thought pattern, you discover that the chains of habit have rested so lightly that you didn't even feel them until now, when they are so strong that you are unable to break them. Sin does not appear to be irresistible—until you want to be free from it. The moment you attack it, you are surprised to find that it is strong. You feel like the man who tried to drain a swamp, not knowing it was fed by an underground stream.

Let's probe more deeply into the real source of our attitudes and behavior. This will take some introspection, but in the end, we will agree that our most basic problem is deep within us. And that is exactly where Christ dwells to help us.

Finding the Source

We think of some sins as "bigger" and others as "smaller," but the distinction between the two is not as significant as we think. A man might remark self-righteously, "I have a bad temper, but you'll never catch me drunk." Or a woman might say, "I struggle with covetousness and discontent, but I'd never commit adultery."

It is true that some sins have worse consequences than others. The thoughts of lust and hatred do not lead to the same social consequences as the acts of adultery and murder. In this sense, sins are not all the same. But from another perspective, essentially all sins are the same because they originate from the same source. We can't rate sins on a scale somewhere between serious and minor. Some sins may seem trifling to us, but that's not how God sees them. The reason? All sins originate from the corruption of our rebellious sinful nature. The New Testament writers often referred to this sinful nature as "the flesh."

Perhaps you are wondering what the flesh is. The flesh is a compulsive inner force inherited from man's fall in Eden that expresses itself in general and specific rebellion against God. In spiritual terms, it is what is often called "the self"—the incurable desire to put personal interests above God's. More particularly, it is manifest as pride, sensuality, covetousness, and so on. By nature we meticulously protect our reputations, we yield to the lusts of the body, and we desire to possess things and people so that our confidence need not be entirely in God.

Read these verses carefully. Do you see the consequences of your own personal sin listed here?

> The acts of the flesh are obvious: sexual immorality, impurity and debauchery; idolatry and witchcraft; hatred, discord, jealousy, fits of rage, selfish ambition, dissensions, factions and envy; drunkenness, orgies, and the like. I warn you, as I did before, that those who live like this will not inherit the kingdom of God (Galatians 5:19-21).

All these behavioral patterns sprout from the same seed—the flesh. We cannot console ourselves by saying that we have one sin but not another. The flesh is a tree with different kinds of branches bearing many kinds of fruit, but all the fruit is sin. In me, it might produce outbursts of anger; in you, it might express itself in selfishness or pride. But both of us, although diverse in behavior and temperament, are being controlled by the flesh. That's why self-righteousness, which always involves a spirit of comparison, is so abhorrent to God. It thrives on a superficial view of sin ("mine is not as bad as yours") and an equally superficial view of God ("surely I'm within reach of His standards").

The Bible puts an end to such vanity. All have sinned, all by nature fulfill the desires of the flesh and of the mind (Romans 3:23). We may think our sin is minor, but it needs the same drastic treatment as the sin of a criminal whose whole life has been twisted by perverse behavior. Our flesh and his are essentially the same—he may not have had our advantages, or perhaps God's grace has restrained us in ways that he did not experience. In either case, our pride and holier-than-thou attitude is sinful.

If this sounds *dis*couraging to those of us who think our sinful habit is of little importance, it ought to be *en*couraging to those of us who see ourselves as beyond hope. Our sinful pattern is no different in principle from that of other people. Some habits are more ingrained than others, but God's remedy for each is much the same.

The flesh, or the self, is so much a part of our thinking that we often do not even recognize its presence. Just in case you think you have escaped its influence, here are some questions to ask yourself, based on questions from a little tract called *Traits of the Self-Life*.[4]

Are you ever conscious of:

A secret spirit of pride; an exalted feeling in view of your success or position because of your good training and appearance, or because of your natural gifts and abilities; an important independent spirit; stiffness and preciseness? Love of human praise, a secret fondness to be noticed; love of supremacy, drawing attention to self in conversation; a swelling out of self when you have had a free time in speaking or praying?

The stirrings of anger or impatience, which, worst of all, you call nervousness or holy indignation; a touchy, sensitive spirit; a disposition that dislikes being contradicted; a desire to throw sharp, heated words at another? Self-will; a stubborn, unteachable spirit; an arguing, talkative spirit; harsh, sarcastic expressions; an unyielding, headstrong disposition; a driving, commanding spirit; a disposition to criticize and pick flaws when set aside and unnoticed; a peevish, fretful spirit; a disposition that loves to be coaxed and humored?

Carnal fear; a man-fearing spirit; a shrinking from reproach and duty; a shrinking from doing your whole duty by those of wealth or position; a fearfulness that someone will offend and drive some prominent person away; a compromising spirit?

A jealous disposition; a secret spirit of envy shut up in your heart; an unpleasant sensation in view of the great prosperity and success of another; a disposition to speak of the faults and failings rather than the gifts and virtues of those more talented and appreciated than yourself?

A dishonest, deceitful disposition; the evading and covering up of the truth; the covering up of your real faults; the leaving of a better impression of yourself than is strictly true; false humility; exaggeration, straining the truth?

Unbelief; a spirit of discouragement in times of pressure and opposition; lack of quietness and confidence in God; lack of faith and trust in God; a disposition to worry and complain in the midst of pain, poverty, or at the dispensations of divine providence; an over-anxious feeling about whether everything will come out all right?

Formality and deadness; lack of concern for lost souls; dryness and indifference; lack of power with God?

God's Solution

God's answer? The *cross*.

Fortunately, God chose to become involved in our predicament. The death of His Son was a solution designed to free us from the frustration of the self-driven life.

Jesus' death accomplished many objectives. The cross is the basis for our forgiveness. It is also the basis for our spiritual freedom—deliverance from our stubborn habits. To appreciate what Christ did, we should become acquainted with two expressions: "in Adam" and "in Christ."

When Adam sinned, the whole human race was plunged into chaos. His descendants have never recovered from the debacle. Our sin nature was inherited from our parents, grandparents, and great grandparents; our ancestry can be traced back to the Garden of Eden.

Just as a child might be born to a family that is in debt (and therefore the child inherits that debt), so we inherit the sinful nature of our forefather, Adam. And when our sin nature is left to itself, it causes us to react in unhealthy ways. ✓

But because of Christ's death, believers are transferred from being "in Adam" to being "in Christ." God breaks our past ties, and Christ becomes our new ancestor. That's why Paul refers—more than a hundred times—to believers as being "in Christ." It's the basis for a whole new approach to life.

All of this seems rather theoretical. Is there some value to this transfer of relationship? After all, after we were converted, we still looked the same, felt the same, and (unfortunately) often acted the same. On the surface, it sounds like being "in Christ" or "in Adam" is only a matter of words.

Not so. Think of a child who is adopted from one family into another. The fact of adoption doesn't change his appearance or his actions. But if he is taken from a family of slaves and adopted into a family of kings, he inherits a new set of relationships. There are new privileges and new responsibilities. That's why Paul could write, "If anyone is in Christ, the new creation has come: The old has gone, the new is here!" (2 Corinthians 5:17).

Here's what happens: God identifies all believers with Christ not in some mystical or theoretical way, but by changing our legal relationships. Before our conversion, we were obligated to obey the sinful impulses of our fallen nature. Even when we became tired of sin and resolved to change, the most we could do was rearrange our lives, but we could not change on the inside.

God has done what we could not do. He has given us a new nature, as well as the personal presence and power of the Holy Spirit so we can say no to our old nature.

To better understand what God has done, imagine yourself as a tenant in an apartment house. The landlord makes your life miserable and charges exorbitant rent. He mistreats you, barges into your apartment, wrecks the furniture, and then blames you for it. One day a new owner buys the apartment complex. You now have a kind landlord who invites you to live in the apartment for free. Not only that, but he fixes all of your furniture as well! You are relieved, grateful, and looking forward to a peaceful future. A few hours later, there is a knock on the door. To your amazement, there is your old landlord, looking as mean and demanding as ever. He threatens you, reminding you that you have rented from him for many years and are obligated to pay him and accept his authority.

What will you do? To resist him on your own is useless—he's more powerful than you are. Your best approach is to remind him you are now under a different management, and he will have to take up your case with the new landlord.

What obligations do you have to your former landlord? He has no more right to demand a payment from you than he does from those whose names appear in an obituary column. That's why Paul exhorts us, "Count yourselves dead to sin but alive in Christ" (Romans 6:11). Your authority to say no to sin is God-given. Although before your conversion you were duty-bound to serve your inherited sin nature, this does not mean that everything you did was evil. Most people are able to control their desires to some extent and are capable of showing compassion and decency.

What it does mean is that we were never free from the futility of unsatisfied desires and frustrated passions. Pride, covetousness, and sensuality were our motivational drives. As believers purchased by God at the cost of His Son, our allegiance is now to Him. By the Holy Spirit, God has given us the power to say no to our old sin nature and yes to our new life in Christ.

Down to Where You Live

How do you apply this knowledge when you want to break a specific habit? First, you must clearly see that in Christ you are already legally dead to your sinful passions, which means you are not a slave to sinful impulses. This is a point many people resist. They think, *I've got to become dead. I've got to pray that God will crucify me so that I will be alive in Christ.* But such thinking is wrong. Being dead to sin is not something that God promises you; it is not an act you beg Him to do. He simply declares it as a fact—it is already accomplished. Your failures and sins cannot change what God has said. Just because you get talked into obeying your former landlord doesn't change the fact you are under a new one. All it means is that you forgot you could confidently say no to the former landlord's extortion.

Let's say, for example, that you are a believer who lives with fear—perhaps a fear of people, disease, or loneliness. You need to recognize those fears as being a bill from your former landlord. You do not have to listen to him—much less do what he suggests. Take the matter up with your new manager. You are no longer duty-bound to the former relationship.

Second, we must admit the need for faith in our daily life. Our identification with Christ is not something that can be proven empirically. It's not like being able to see with our own eyes that the sun is shining. And even if the fact we are in Christ could be proven by our experience, we would still be in trouble. An honest look at our lives hardly supports the idea that we are dead to sin and alive to God. But once we understand, with the Holy Spirit's help, that our ties with sin have already been broken, we begin to see that God has not deceived us. When we shift our attention to the completed work of the cross and insist on our privileges, our old self surrenders to God's authority. Through faith and faith alone we personalize our victory.

Let me add that freedom from sin is never automatic. Every inch is contested. No one ever falls into maturity, even though from a positional standpoint we are already complete in Christ. One danger of reading a book like this is that we may tend to look for formulas or a new spiritual technique for righteous living. But there is no substitute for waiting before God, reading His Word, and then obeying the truth He has revealed.

Years ago, archeologists found grain buried in the tombs of the Egyptian Pharaohs. Incredibly, when they planted the seeds and exposed them to both water and sunshine, they grew! For some 4000 years these seeds gave no evidence of life, but under the right conditions, the life that was dormant grew.

Jesus said that "unless a kernel of wheat falls to the ground and dies, it remains only a single seed. But if it dies, it produces many seeds" (John 12:23-24). The Holy Spirit abides within all true believers in Christ, but that power is only experienced as we die to our own agendas and selfish ambitions. We have to come to the place where we say, "In Christ I died, and now in Christ I live."

The Christian life is a growing relationship. Applying the cross to your life is not something you do once. Nor is it sufficient to do it every week or even once a day. It is a moment-by-moment, daily process. As you develop sensitivity to the Holy Spirit's work in you, you will find that saying no to the flesh and yes to Christ will be the pattern of your life.

In the next chapter, you will learn more about how you can personalize Christ's victory through the power of the Holy Spirit.

ACTION STEP: Stop now to give thanks to God that in Christ, your need for spiritual resources has been met. Right now, give praise to Him that you no longer have any obligation to your former landlord.

Questions for Personal Reflection or Group Study

1. If you have not already done so, now is the time to take stock of your life, asking what behavior patterns or thoughts you must allow God to begin to change.

2. Read Romans chapters 6 through 8 carefully. Underline each instance in which Paul uses the expression "free from sin" or its equivalent. In each case, find what Paul gives as the basis for your freedom.

3. The more clearly you see the wide-ranging benefits of the cross, the more you will develop a life of habitual praise. What are some things you can praise God for right now? Begin this habit by thanking God multiple times through the day for the victory Christ accomplished on your behalf.

4. Begin each day by giving it to God. Take time to:
   a. Give thanks that Christ has already conquered the problems you will face that day.
   b. Accept by faith the victory Christ won at the cross—before you are tempted to sin.

CHAPTER 6

The Power of the Holy Spirit

If you feel defeated and spiritually
weak, I have good news for you:
The Holy Spirit is a helper you can count on.

Years ago, when slavery was officially abolished in Jamaica, some of the slaves in the remote areas did not yet know of their freedom. Years after their release had been announced, they still continued to serve their masters, oblivious to the fact that they were legally free. Their owners kept the news from the slaves as long as possible, hoping to extract every ounce of work from their captives. The slaves wouldn't have had to put up with the drudgery of their labors—except for their ignorance of the facts.

Jesus Christ issues a proclamation of liberty to every believer. We've already learned that our union with Him qualifies us to share His victory. But precisely how is His victory translated into our experience? The answer lies in the personal ministry of the Holy Spirit. He communicates Christ's strength to us. He satisfies our spiritual thirst. Let's consider what Jesus had to say about the Spirit's ministry.

When Jesus attended the Feast of Tabernacles at Jerusalem, He was deeply bothered by the emptiness of the rituals the Jewish people dutifully performed. Bible scholars tell us that on that day, a group of white-robed priests went down to the pool of Siloam. They filled their jars with water from the pool, and then walked back to the temple and poured out the water in the presence of the people. This symbolic act was to remind them of how God had supplied the Israelites' need for water during their wandering in the wilderness.

This ceremony was a beautiful reminder of what God had done, but the people missed its spiritual meaning—that God wanted to satisfy their spiritual thirst as well. Scripture says:

> On the last and greatest day of the festival, Jesus stood and said in a loud voice, "Let anyone who is thirsty come to me and drink. Whoever believes in me, as Scripture has said, rivers of living water will flow from within them." By this he meant the Spirit, whom those who believed in him were later to receive. Up to that time the Spirit had not been given, since Jesus had not yet been glorified (John 7:37-39).

Jesus was predicting the coming of the new age in which the Holy Spirit would be poured out upon God's people.

Notice carefully that the basis of the gift of the Spirit is the glorification of Jesus Christ. The Spirit, Jesus said, could not be given to His people until He was glorified. God doesn't give the Spirit to His people because they agonize for Him or fast. Rather, the Spirit is given because Jesus has ascended into heaven. In the Old Testament era, the Spirit's work was limited; after Christ's ascension, the Spirit was given to every believer. Listen to the words of Jesus to His followers: "Truly I tell you, it is for your good that I am going away. Unless I go away, the Advocate will not come to you; but if I go, I will send him to you" (John 16:7). Jesus could not give the Spirit to the church until He left this earth physically. He had to be glorified before the Spirit could descend upon His people.

Think of it this way: Jesus Christ's death on the cross is the basis for our forgiveness. Because He took our penalty, we can receive forgiveness of sins without strings attached. The only requirement is trust—a transfer of our faith from ourselves to Jesus alone. Similarly, the basis on which the Holy Spirit is given is Jesus' ascension and glorification. We don't have to beg for forgiveness, nor do we need to agonize for the Spirit; the Water of Life is also free, and is received by faith.

Ever since Christ was glorified and the Spirit was given on the day of Pentecost, every believer has received Him (Romans 8:9; 1 Corinthians 6:19). There is no need for striving, anxiety, or a feeling that we are unworthy to receive Him. He is waiting to quench our thirst, but His control in our lives is never automatic.

How Do We Receive the Spirit's Power?

Do you know the reaction of many Christians when someone talks to them about walking in the fullness of the Holy Spirit? They say, "That's great for others, but I'm not good enough. I don't qualify. If I were more dedicated and spent more time in Bible reading and prayer, I might eventually be worthy to walk in the Spirit."

But they've got it backward. The Holy Spirit is not given to those who have it all together spiritually; He is given to enable us to get it together spiritually! I'm struck by Paul's words: "So I say, walk by the Spirit, and you will not gratify the desires of the flesh" (Galatians 5:16). Notice the sequence. Paul did not say that if we stop carrying out the desires of the flesh we will walk in the Spirit. Rather, he said that if we walk in the Spirit, we will not fulfill the desires of the flesh!

This order makes an incredible difference. Christians often ignore any thought of walking by the Spirit because they think they are not good enough. Their life is too filled with fleshly struggles. But that's like refusing to accept medicine until we get well and feel worthy of it. The whole purpose of medicine is to enable us to get well. It is given to the sick, not the healthy. In the same way, the Spirit is given to enable us to break sin's hold on us. We don't have to do that on our own before we receive the Spirit's power.

Imagine someone saying, "I'm not good enough to be saved; I'm going to wait until I get myself together before I come to Christ." We would quickly point out that salvation is designed for sinners. None of us is ever good enough to be saved; we are saved because of God's great generosity in Jesus Christ. People who say they aren't good enough are missing the point of Jesus' death.

But the same applies to the Holy Spirit. As Jesus' death gives us forgiveness, so Jesus' ascension and glorification give us the Holy Spirit. And the coming of the Holy Spirit into our lives is not just a window dressing. He indwells us so that we might allow Him to control us.

I believe that we have often made the requirements for walking in the Spirit too complicated. We've stressed dedication, surrender, and discipline as prerequisites to receiving and walking in the power of the Holy Spirit. When I read books that give seven steps to the filling of the Spirit or others that condense it to four, I find myself asking, "Can any one of us be sure we have fully carried out all of these requirements?" Is not the Spirit's power given to sinners to enable them to be yielded and disciplined, rather than expecting all of these characteristics from them first?

Notice Jesus' words: "Let anyone who is thirsty come to me and drink" (John 7:37). The only requirement is a thirst that will draw us to come to Him. We don't have to be supersaints, just thirsty sinners. That's why Jesus could offer living water to a woman who had had five husbands and was living in a common-law marriage. He promised that from within her would burst forth living water that would quench her emotional and spiritual thirst (John 4:10-14).

Are you thirsty? Do you feel, as I have often felt, like an apple tree trying to grow in a desert? Then you are a candidate for the Spirit's life and power.

Life in the Spirit

There is a direct connection between walking in the Spirit and breaking a sinful habit. Today, many people suffer from drug addiction. Perhaps they began getting high just for kicks, or because they wanted to look cool, but now they are hooked. Drugs as we know them today were not available in New Testament times, but back then many people were addicted to wine, which led Paul to write to the believers in Ephesus, "Do not get drunk on wine, which leads to debauchery. Instead, be filled with the Spirit" (Ephesians. 5:18). To those who are struggling with an addiction of any kind, the Bible offers a different master: Be controlled by the Spirit rather than drugs or alcohol or any other stubborn habit. The Spirit's control will replace sin's control. His power is greater than the power of all your sin put together.

Perhaps you're wondering at this point, "Okay, how do I get hold of this power?" You begin by clearing the deck. Confess your sin—and the sin must be confessed—and receive God's forgiveness. Claim 1 John 1:9: "If we confess our sins, he is faithful and just and will forgive us our sins and purify us from all unrighteousness."

Then remember that the Holy Spirit desires to energize you. Don't ever think that He is reluctant, waiting to be coaxed into the driver's seat of your life. He became a resident with the express purpose of becoming president. But He will not exercise His power apart from your faith. If you ask Him to control you, believe that He will.

Maybe you feel unworthy, or perhaps you think that there will be a more convenient time to yield yourself to the Spirit. F.B. Meyer is reported to have said of his experience: "I left the prayer meeting and crept away into the lane praying, 'O Lord, if there was ever a man who needs the power of the Holy Spirit, it is I. But I do not know how to receive Him. I am too tired, too worn, too nervously run down to agonize.' Then a voice said to me, 'As you took forgiveness from the hand of the dying Christ, take the Holy Spirit from the hand of the living Christ.'" Meyer said from then onward, he took continuously of the Holy Spirit.

How were you saved? By depending on the *death* of Jesus Christ. How do you receive the power of the Spirit? By depending on the *ascension* of Jesus Christ. Both come by faith. That's why Paul wrote, "As you therefore have received Christ Jesus the Lord, so walk in Him, rooted and built up in Him" (Colossians 2:6-7 NKJV).

You receive the Spirit's filling by faith, not by having a particular feeling. Some Christians wrongly believe that the filling of the Spirit is a sensation. They expect waves of love, an overwhelming sense of peace, or the ability to speak in strange languages. Theirs is a fleshly desire to walk by sight, not by faith. We find it difficult to take God at His Word, and like the Pharisees, we ask for a sign that we might believe.

God, however, delights when we believe in Him without demanding emotional crutches. Just as a new believer needs to receive God's promises—apart from feelings—so we daily need to receive the power of the Holy Spirit—apart from feelings.

Living by Praise

You will be greatly helped in accepting the Spirit's control if you learn the power of praise. "Those who sacrifice thank offerings honor me, and to the blameless I will show my salvation" (Psalm 50:23). Paul put it this way: "Give thanks in all circumstances; for this is God's will for you in Christ Jesus" (1 Thessalonians 5:18).

When we read these exhortations to giving thanks and praise, we tend to make two very common errors. One is to think we should thank and praise God only for the good things He gives us—health, food, clothes, and other blessings. The second is to think that we should praise God only when we feel like doing so. But Paul wrote, "Give thanks in *all* circumstances." That means every single one, whether pleasant or painful. It's only when we choose to give praise in the rough spots of life that we begin to see them from God's perspective. Furthermore, if we don't give thanks in all things, we are living in unbelief, for we are assuming that our circumstances are not controlled by a God who loves us. I'm not saying that you should give thanks for sin, but you can thank God for how He will use that sin to teach, rebuke, or humble you.

Also, you can learn to give thanks even when you don't feel particularly thankful. If God gives a command, He expects obedience, whether you are in the mood to obey or not. Thankfulness, like forgiveness, is not an emotion. Thankfulness is an intelligent response of gratitude to God, based on His Word. It is your determination to be obedient.

Here's what to do: Name your sin, and give thanks to God that in Jesus you already are victorious over it. When Jesus died on the cross, He provided forgiveness and freedom. Thank God for both, saying something like this: "Father, I thank You that I am in Christ. I thank

You that my position is secure and immovable. I thank You that in Him I've already won the victory over the sin that besets me. And I thank You that I am free." In time, your experience will catch up with what God has already given you in Christ.

I'm not talking about a once-and-for-all act of thanksgiving. David wrote, "I will extol the LORD at all times; his praise will always be on my lips" (Psalm 34:1). But how does praise become a way of life, a daily habit, more regular than tying your shoes or combing your hair?

You don't learn to express ongoing praise in a day, especially since you may have been complaining for years. New habits take time to develop. But you can begin today, and practice tomorrow, and the next day, until it becomes part of you. "Let the message of Christ dwell among you richly as you teach and admonish one another with all wisdom through psalms, hymns, and songs from the Spirit, singing to God with gratitude in your hearts" (Colossians 3:16).

The Holy Spirit is willing. Are you?

ACTION STEP: As you make your way through each day, which do you focus on more: walking in the Spirit, or eliminating specific sins from your life? Remember, Paul wrote that as you walk in the Spirit, you will not fulfill the desires of the flesh. Take time now to thank God for giving you a permanent helper, the Holy Spirit, and that in Christ, you are already victorious over sin.

Questions for Personal Reflection or Group Study

1. In Galatians 5:22-23, Paul lists nine fruit of the Spirit. Which two are the most evident in your life? Which two are the least evident? Take some time now to ask God to help you improve in the areas in which you are lacking.

2. Think specifically of ways in which the fruit of the Spirit can be further developed in your life. These questions might help:

   a. What obstacles in your life hinder the ministry of the Spirit? Unconfessed sin? Strained personal relationships? Lack of commitment? Little or no time spent in Bible reading or prayer?

   b. Have you ever asked God to control you with His Spirit? Remember, we often have not because we ask not (James 4:2). Why not simply thank Him for His control each day, knowing that He will give you strength?

3. The most important ingredient in releasing the Spirit's power in our lives is faith. Our faith is strengthened by (a) making the Word of God the focus of our attention, and (b) developing the habit of praise. Write down some creative ways to make these practices a part of your daily activity.

4. Regardless of your current life circumstances, spend some time in prayer right now thanking God for who He is and what He has done for you. Ask Him to increase the thankfulness aspect of your daily prayer life.

CHAPTER 7

The Renewing of Your Mind

You are not what you think you are;
but what you think, you are!

Have you given your anxiety to God only to find an hour later that the weight is back on your shoulders? Do you ask God to control your temper, but still blow your top? Have you prayed not to lust, or even reckoned yourself dead to sinful impulses, only to find that tall blonde from the coffee shop walking around in your mind again the next morning?

We surrender ourselves to God, but so soon and so easily revert to our old habits. We mean well, yet fare so poorly. Why?

Jesus told a story that illustrates the most important single principle in breaking a sinful habit. There once was a man who had been inhabited by a demon. The demon caused the man to do awful things and controlled every area of his life. But one day, the demon was expelled, and the man danced with joy. The evil spirit then passed through waterless places, seeking rest. Finding none, it decided to return to its original house, right in the center of the poor man's life. To its satisfaction, the demon saw that its original living space was unoccupied. It then found seven other spirits even more evil than itself to go and live there with it. Sadly, the man, who just a short time earlier had been dancing with joy, was now worse off than before (Luke 11:24-26).

Why did this man fail in his quest for freedom? He didn't understand the principle of replacement. None of us can overcome evil by simply renouncing it. Rather, we can only do so by substituting good in its place. Sinful habits cannot be broken without replacing them with righteous ones.

For example, try this simple experiment: Think of the number eight. Have you visualized it? If so, exercise your willpower and stop thinking of the number eight right now.

Were you able to do it? Of course not. At least, I'm still thinking about that number. Can we, by sheer willpower, stop thinking about the number eight once it has been mentioned? By no means. Trying to push it out of our minds actually causes us to focus our attention on it all the more.

That is a picture of what happens when we try to overcome sin. We may get on our knees and ask God to take the desire away, and we may determine not to think those lurid or greedy thoughts. But then they surface again. We resist them once more, trying desperately to push them out of our minds. But we are trapped. Try as we might, we just can't get those thoughts to budge.

Can we really be free? Yes, we can control those thoughts, but not by trying to stop thinking about them! To simply resist evil is to make it grow stronger. Our determination not to think lustful thoughts only reinforces them in our thought patterns.

How, then, can we be free? Let's return to our experiment once more and think of the number eight. Although we can't stop thinking about it by sheer resistance, we can push that number out of our minds quite easily. Here's how: Think about one or two bits of information about your mother. Reminisce about your place in the family, whether you are still connected with it or disconnected. Concentrate on this new information, and you'll stop thinking of the number eight.

You can handle sinful thought patterns in the same way. Fear, lust, covetousness—all of these can be squeezed out of your mind by turning your thoughts to the Scriptures. Freedom comes by filling your mind with God's thoughts (Romans 12:1-2; Philippians 4:8).

I know a young man whose wife died of cancer. She suffered intensely during the last weeks of her life. Yet she and her husband were able to accept this tragedy without bitterness or the slightest trace of self-pity. I asked John, "Why were you and your wife able to accept this so well? Weren't you ever resentful and angry at God through this ordeal?" His reply: "Yes, we had moments like that. But when they came, I read the Scriptures to my wife. Then we bought the whole New Testament on CD, and we played it in our house, hour after hour." That was the secret—expelling angry and anxious thoughts by filling the mind with the Word of God.

What is the best way to take air out of a bottle? Possibly someone could suggest that we build an elaborate vacuum pump to suck out the air. But there is a simpler solution. If we fill the bottle with water, the air has to leave.

To diffuse the power of sin, you need to have your thought patterns replaced by the Word of God. Every temptation, vice, or sinister motive comes to you by your thoughts; these must be brought under the control of the Holy Spirit. Paul wrote, "Do not conform to the pattern of this world, but be transformed by the renewing of your mind. Then you will be able to test and approve what God's will is—his good, pleasing and perfect will" (Romans 12:2). The difference between worldliness and godliness is a renewed mind. This old adage puts it straight: You aren't what you think you are; but what you *think*, you are!

Let us suppose we could flash all the thoughts we had last week on a giant screen. Not a one of us would like to have others view the details! Yet, discouraging though this would be, *that* is who we really are! Our thoughts not only shape our life; they *are* our life.

Somewhere I read about a man recently released from prison who was having difficulty adjusting to his freedom. He tried this experiment: He took a glass bottle with a distinct shape and crammed it full of wires—some small, and some large. After some time had passed, he smashed the bottle with a hammer. The result? Most of the wires retained the shape of the bottle. Those wires had to be straightened out, one by one.

That man discovered that it is possible to be technically free and still retain the traits of bondage. Even though a person is liberated, he or she must adjust to freedom and carefully dismantle the habits of the past.

As a believer, you are legally free in Christ, but you can still be enslaved by the fantasies of the flesh and the vices of the world. You can yield, surrender, and pray, but your mind will revert to familiar territory as soon as your experience wears thin. To break this self-defeating cycle, you need to outline a specific strategy for experiencing the freedom you have in Christ and accepting the victory that is legally yours.

Prepare for Battle

Is this really possible? Yes, but not without locking horns with wicked spiritual forces. Read carefully Paul's words:

> Though we live in the world, we do not wage war as the world does. The weapons we fight with are not the weapons of the world. On the contrary, they have divine power to demolish strongholds. We demolish arguments and every pretension that sets itself up against the knowledge of God, and we take captive every thought to make it obedient to Christ (2 Corinthians 10:3-5).

You have the spiritual artillery needed to destroy the fortresses of the mind. Vain reasoning, powerful imaginations, and perverted attitudes can be routed. You have the spiritual equipment to track down your thoughts and make them captive to Christ.

Military moves are made according to a determined strategy. Weapons need to be understood before they are used. In this battle with Satan and evil, you need to know the strategy and to be well acquainted with your weapons. Specifically, how can you do this?

First, you must identify the thoughts that you want to replace. You must name the fantasies, imaginations, and attitudes that you want to be rid of. To say, "I want to be a better Christian" or "I want to be more joyful" will not do. Generalities are no good. You must be specific.

I assume that you know the sins in your life that won't budge. In fact, if you have participated in all the study questions in this book to this point, you should already have a very good idea of your chief struggles. Now, take a sheet of paper and jot down which thought patterns have to go. Don't skip this step! Few people take the time to write down their goals, and fewer still actually accomplish what they haven't written down, so it is very important to write down the aspects of your life that you want to change.

Second, be prepared for the discipline of spiritual warfare. The world, the flesh, and the devil do not surrender without a struggle. Psalm 1:2 describes what it takes for a person to be blessed by God: "His delight is in the law of the LORD, and in His law he meditates day and night" (Psalm 1:2 NKJV).

Sometimes we are told, "We are in a spiritual battle. As soldiers of the cross, we must be disciplined; we must put effort and sacrifice into the Christian life." Then perhaps a week later, someone else tells us the opposite: "I was working too hard at being a Christian. God showed me that I had to just relax—that I had to *rest* in the Lord."

Though these viewpoints appear contradictory, they are not. *Only a Christian who is disciplined in the Word of God can rest in the Lord.* Yes, we can cease our striving and learn to relax in the confidence that God is equal to every situation. But a lazy, undisciplined Christian cannot do so; he falls apart at the seams when tragedy strikes. The believer who is "like a tree planted by the rivers of water" (Psalm 1:3 KJV) is the one who meditates in the law of God every free moment (verse 2). His thoughts turn to the Word of God like steel to a magnet.

Declaring war on your thought life means that you must set aside time every morning to begin your offensive attack. I suggest 20 minutes as a minimum. Meditation in the Scriptures requires effort; nothing worth having can be achieved without exertion.

You've heard the cliché "A chapter a day keeps the devil away." Don't you believe it. You can read a chapter of the Bible with your mind on tomorrow's business deal or with a heart full of revenge. Real meditation requires quality time. You must assimilate a passage and give it your unhurried attention. Find a truth in God's Word that you can think about all day.

Finally, be prepared to memorize the Word of God. "I have hidden your word in my heart that I might not sin against you" (Psalm 119:11). Rather than memorizing verses at random, take your list of troublesome thought patterns and find Scripture passages that speak directly to them. Specific examples are given at the end of this chapter. Memorize these verses so that you have them at your fingertips during the day—you'll need them. The only alternative to memorizing verses is typing them out on small note cards so that you can have them on hand for immediate reference. These are the passages that God will use to demolish the present strongholds of your mind and construct a new edifice.

Use Your Artillery

So far you've identified your sins, you've decided to set aside 20 minutes for God each morning, and you've even gotten some passages of Scripture to work with. Now what? What should you do tomorrow morning? Your strategy should begin the moment you awake. Those moments between waking up and getting your feet on the floor are crucial. The seeds of discouragement, anger, and lust begin there. While still in bed, thank God for the rest He has given you. I personally pray, "Today I get up in the name of the Father, the Son, and the Holy Spirit." Consciously commit your mind, opportunities, and time to Him. Remind yourself of God's promises. Here are a few:

No word from God will ever fail (Luke 1:37).

We know that in all things God works for the good of those who love him, who have been called according to his purpose (Romans 8:28).

I can do all this through him who gives me strength (Philippians 4:13).

Reminding yourself of God's promises gives you the proper perspective on life.

Then after you're out of bed and reasonably awake (I need coffee—lots of coffee—to get my mind in gear), read a chapter from the Bible, observing what God is saying to you.

Then spend some time preparing your mind for the particular temptation you are likely to face that day. Let's suppose your boss habitually irritates you. An hour after you arrive at work, you wish you could scream. If you wait until your boss shouts at you before you decide how you will respond, you'll probably react in anger. Use the Word of God in anticipation. During your time with God in the morning, recite the verses you have memorized and claim Christ's victory before your boss blows his fuse.

The same principle applies whether you're struggling with an eating disorder, pornography, tobacco, or alcohol. Claim God's promises for that particular day. Tell Him that with His help, you resolve to choose Him rather than the world.

But remember, if you wait until temptation arrives to decide how you will react, you've waited too long! Choose beforehand to claim God's promises for whatever circumstances you expect to encounter.

Then, during the day, learn to obey the first promptings of the Holy Spirit. If you are tempted to enjoy a sensual fantasy, deal with those thoughts immediately. Each of us knows when we let our minds skip across that invisible line into forbidden territory. The moment we do so, we sense we are violating the purity the Holy Spirit desires. That is the moment to say, "I reject these thoughts in the name of

Jesus." And then quote the passages of Scripture you have learned for that temptation. With time, your sensitivity to the Holy Spirit will develop.

Most important, learn to switch topics on the flesh and the devil. Remember the experiment at the beginning of this chapter? We couldn't stop thinking of the number eight, no matter how hard we tried. Not until we switched our thoughts to another topic could we get the number eight out of our minds.

You can do this with any temptation you face. Simply use your temptation as an alarm system—a signal to give praise to God. If, for example, you fear cancer (because one out of every four people in the United States will get cancer, your fears may have a statistical basis), use that fear as an opportunity to give glory to God. Quote Romans 8:35-39 or read Psalms 103, 144, or 145. Then thank God for all the blessings you have in Christ. Thank Him for forgiveness, for His sovereignty, power, and love. In this way, your stumbling block will be changed into a stepping-stone. You'll be praising rather than pouting.

While I was writing this chapter, a woman called on the phone to ask me to pray that she would overcome her battle with smoking. She had tried to be free, but hadn't succeeded. I gave her several suggestions; one was to accept the desire for a cigarette as a reminder that it was time to read a chapter of the Bible and give praise to God. She was to resist that desire by focusing on God and His power. Eventually, she would learn that she did not have to yield to this temptation; the very struggle would become God's way of building discipline into her life.

Unfortunately, the more I probed, the more I realized there was a whole cluster of other issues in her life that vied for resolution. As mentioned in a previous chapter, it is difficult to tackle one destructive habit while planning to tolerate other such habits at the same time. God intends to change the core of our motivations and values.

If your problem is unhealthy eating—whether you eat too much or too little—decide that your urges will be a reminder to divert your attention to God's Word. Knowing you will be tempted, develop a strategy in advance. Memorize a verse of Scripture, pray for your missionary friends, sing a hymn of praise. By outlining and following a specific strategy to resist temptation, you will eventually be freed from its grip.

Finally, do not be discouraged by the frequency of your battles with the same temptation. If you have lived a long time with sinful thought patterns, the strongholds of your imagination will not be easily toppled. Furthermore, you must recognize the possibility that you are not merely confronting yourself, but satanic forces as well. Satan's most-used weapon is discouragement. After you have rejected insidious thoughts, he delights in having them pop back into your mind. Since his activity has become so overt in our society, a later chapter will give specific instruction on how to confront these forces. For now, let me say that the most important insulation you have against satanic attack is personal righteousness—confessing and forsaking sin. And as you apply the above principles consistently, Satan and his forces will be weakened. Eventually they will flee.

How long does it take for the mind to be renewed? That depends. Some Christians who apply these principles recognize a noticeable difference within a week. Others who are steeped in decades of sin may need months before they can say, "I am free!" And, of course, no one reaches perfection. The more we meditate on the Word, the more clearly we see new areas of our lives that need to be changed. Some subtle motives aren't detected until after we've had long exposure to the light of God's Word.

I once counseled a man who struggled with homosexual temptations but was freed to live a life of celibacy realizing that he would have to live a life that was pleasing to God even if he lived with unfulfilled desires. The Word of God changed his attitudes. "Now," he says, "God is changing my desires. During the process, I am committed to celibacy, a life that honors the Lord." He is proof of what God can do in the life of anyone who persistently meditates on His Word and applies it directly to areas of spiritual conflict.

I'm convinced that God intends us to be free from mental bondage. His Word is the resource by which our thoughts can become obedient to Him. Even Christ, the eternal Son of God, "learned obedience from what he suffered" (Hebrews 5:8). And if He, the Son, sets you free, you will be free indeed (John 8:36).

> **ACTION STEP:** The following Scripture references can be used to begin the process of bringing your thoughts under the control of the Holy Spirit. Additional passages can be found through careful reading of the Scriptures along with the use of a concordance or *Nave's Topical Bible*.

Covetousness
Psalm 119:36; Luke 12:15; Colossians 3:1-2,5-6; Philippians 4:11-12; 1 Timothy 6:6; Hebrews 13:5

Pride
Proverbs 16:18; Galatians 6:3,14; James 4:6; 1 Peter 5:5-6

Lack of discipline
Romans 12:11; 1 Corinthians 9:26-27; Philippians 4:12-13; Hebrews 6:12

Lust
Romans 6:11-12; 2 Corinthians 10:4-5; Ephesians 4:22-24; Philippians 4:8; 1 Peter 2:11

Anger
Psalm 37:8; Proverbs 14:29; 16:32; Ephesians 4:26,31; Colossians 3:8; James 1:19-20

Worry
Matthew 6:25-34; Philippians 4:6; 1 Peter 5:7

Bitterness
Ephesians 4:31-32; Hebrews 12:15

Unhealthy Eating
Judges 3:14-22; Proverbs 23:20-21; 1 Corinthians 9:27; 10:31-33; Philippians 4:12

Questions for Personal Reflection or Group Study

1. How much time do you really spend in God's Word on a daily basis? Be honest. Admitting your need in this area of your life is the first step toward positive growth. Now spend some time in prayer and ask God to increase your desire to meditate on the Scriptures daily.

2. Earlier in the chapter we talked about replacing one set of thoughts with another. What are some things you can think about as a means of overcoming temptation? Which Scripture passages should you memorize so you can think of them clearly during times of temptation? Is there a trusted friend or someone you can call, day or night, when temptation begins to overcome you?

3. Spiritual warfare is real. Take some time right now to name the specific areas in which you have been struggling. Pray that God would help you overcome these trials, and that the blood of Christ would help you stand against the evil one.

CHAPTER 8

Living with Your Feelings

Our faith must triumph over our feelings.

Today's generation places a high priority on feeling good. If you watch the ads on TV, you know how to reach this goal. First, you must surround yourself with the right things—the latest styles in clothing, an expensive new car, a home in the right neighborhood, just to start with. Second, you should look attractive; if necessary, have plastic surgery so you can turn heads in any room. Finally, you should not worry how your actions will affect those around you. "If it feels good, do it!"

It is significant that the first sin ever committed was caused by someone choosing to follow personal feelings instead of God's commands. The fruit of this tree, Eve was told, would satisfy her hunger in ways that the fruit of the other trees could not. She would gain wisdom and become queen of her own domain. Little did she know the consequences that would result from her decision. Ever since that time, people have been driven by feelings or desires even when they are not in harmony with God's commands.

Of course, feelings in and of themselves are not evil. God created us with the ability to feel pain and joy; Jesus Himself is "touched with the feeling of our infirmities" (Hebrews 4:15 KJV). To stoically ignore our feelings or reject them out of hand is to invite callousness and indifference. Paul condemned the wicked who were no longer capable of compassion, who were past feeling (Ephesians 4:19). But our feelings are not a fully reliable guide for behavior. Many feelings must be restrained, both for our good and the good of others.

Our will must provide a check on the stream of emotions that ebb and flow through our being. If we follow our feelings wherever they lead, we will be fulfilling virtually every wanton desire. Of course, all of us have feelings that are a part of being human, but if these feelings rage out of control, they can result either in anger, bitterness, or depression, in which case special counseling may be necessary.

In this chapter we will discuss self-control and our need to submit our desires to God's lordship. When Jesus spoke to His tempter, He said, "Man shall not live on bread alone, but on every word that comes from the mouth of God" (Matthew 4:4). He was suggesting the principle of balance—of a life under the authority of the revealed Word of God.

Pitfalls of Living by Feelings

Before I suggest how you can cope with your emotions, I want you to consider what happens when you live by the dictates of your hunches and whims. A life based on desires is an invitation to the sin of disobedience. Often our feelings run counter to what God requires. In fact, most sinful habits are developed by simply following the path of least resistance, by doing whatever we feel like doing. Many of our struggles can be traced to sensuality, and by that I mean being controlled by our physical senses. This spawns defeat, self-absorption, and unbelief.

Many people who think they cannot obey God's commandments simply don't feel like obeying. Occasionally they have days when they wake up wanting to do what God requires, but not often. Our fallen human nature never feels like obeying God; usually it wants to do its own thing. This attitude comes from Satan as he suggests to us—as he did to Eve—that God has asked us to obey commands that we cannot or need not keep. If we think we can't obey God until we *feel* like it, we will never get off the ground in our spiritual lives.

Let's be specific. In his book on overcoming difficulties in marriage, biblical counselor Jay Adams wrote of a counseling situation in which all love had been drained from the marriage and the partners had already agreed to a divorce. Neither one had committed a serious sin against the marriage. They just didn't *feel* in love anymore. They went to the counselor hoping he would confirm their decision that because they no longer had feelings for each other, they should divorce. The couple was shocked when the counselor said, "If you don't love each other, there is only one thing to do: You will have to *learn* to love one another." Both the husband and wife were stunned. "How can you learn to love someone? You can't produce feelings out of thin air!"

The counselor explained that in the Bible, God commands us to love one another. When the husband was told that he should love his wife as Christ loved the church, he gasped. He could never do that. But the counselor persisted. He explained that the husband should begin on a lesser level. The Bible also commands us to love our neighbor, and because his wife was his closest neighbor, he should love her. Even so, the husband rejected the idea that he could love his wife that way. Then the counselor explained that he was still not off the hook, for God had commanded us to love even our enemies!

This couple had made a common error: They had equated love with feelings. In the Bible, love is not a feeling. We can learn to love, even though we begin with little or no emotional impetus. In other words, we can *choose* to love. And God gives us the grace to do so.

Love is not an emotion; neither is forgiveness. The Bible commands us to put away all bitterness (Ephesians 4:31); we are to forgive others whether they solicit our forgiveness or not (verse 32). Yet many Christians believe that they can't forgive until they feel like it. They think that if they forgive when they don't feel like it, they are hypocritical.

However, if forgiveness were an emotion, God would be commanding us to do the impossible. We cannot switch our emotions on and off. We cannot develop the right feelings on our own. But God is not mocking us when He tells us to forgive; we can choose to do so, whether we feel like it or not. Never try to skirt God's commands under the pretense that you don't feel like obeying Him.

A second danger of living by feelings is that you may tend to derive your doctrine from feelings. If you believe God is with you just because "He feels so close," you will also believe there are days when He forsakes you because "He feels so far away." The assurance of God's presence does not come by feelings, but by faith (Hebrews 13:5). Fortunately, you don't always have to feel God's presence to be in fellowship with Him and to make spiritual progress.

The apostle Paul, who by any standard lived a successful, victorious Christian life, had his bad days. "We do not want you to be uninformed, brothers and sisters, about the troubles we experienced in the province of Asia. We were under great pressure, far beyond our ability to endure, so that we despaired of life itself" (2 Corinthians 1:8). Have you ever been restless, unable to control your fluctuating emotions? Paul wrote that he had no rest in his spirit until Titus came to him with some good news from the church (2:13).

Even more surprising is the testimony of Jesus. As He approached the cross, He was tempted to call a halt to the whole plan of redemption. He was deeply vexed in spirit. "Now my soul is troubled, and what shall I say? 'Father, save me from this hour'? No, it was for this very reason I came to this hour. Father, glorify your name!" (John 12:27-28).

Jesus' agony in Gethsemane is well documented. His soul was troubled "to the point of death" (Matthew 26:38). Emotionally, He shrank from the pain and torture that were ahead and asked if it were possible that the cup of suffering might pass from Him (verse 39). All these emotional upheavals took place in the God-man, the One who lived perfectly, sinlessly.

Now, it is often true that depression is the result of sin—particularly anger, self-pity, or unresolved guilt. For example, a woman who had seen half a dozen counselors could not cope with the intense periods of depression she faced. Despite hours of counsel, she had withheld one important bit of information—namely, that as a teenage girl, she had given birth to a baby and had killed it to avoid the stigma that comes from engaging in an illicit sexual affair. When she finally admitted her sin, confessed it, and accepted God's forgiveness, the depression left. Self-pity, hostility, and warped values can have the same effect. That is why those who think they have emotional problems often discover that their problems are not really emotional after all. Indeed, their emotions are working only too well. Their emotional struggles are often symptomatic of unresolved guilt from sin that they have been unwilling to face.

However, at times you may experience emotional turbulence that may not be related to any particular sin. The cause may be physiological, or perhaps Satan is trying to disrupt your fellowship with God. At any rate, this point needs emphasis: You do not need to experience a steady stream of placid emotional feelings in order to know that you are walking with God.

Emotions fluctuate. They are perhaps only a little more dependable than the weather. Today you might feel great, but tonight you might not be able to sleep, and tomorrow life may seem pointless. It is in the difficult moments of life that you come to recognize whether you have learned to walk by faith or you are still dependent on emotional sight. Personally, I'm glad that my acceptance before God is unrelated to the way I feel! Sometimes our feelings tell us lies.

A third consequence of living by feelings is that you develop the sin of procrastination. It's time to visit a friend in the hospital, write a letter or email, or do some chores at home. You know what you ought to do, but for some mysterious reason you can't seem to get started. You stall, putter around, watch TV. In short, you procrastinate. Why?

There may be several reasons. You may feel frustrated because the task seems overwhelming. Or you may feel inferior, thinking you are unable to do the job as well as someone else. So you sit around, waiting for the magic moment when suddenly everything will fall into place. But those magic moments never come, and your responsibilities never go away.

The result is that you begin to feel guilty for not doing what you know you should. Putting matters off does not relieve tension, but increases it. Perhaps the most tragic consequence of living according to feelings is that such a life ends up being self-defeating. It seems reasonable to believe that the sure path to happiness is to be able to do whatever you feel like doing. But if you follow that reasoning, eventually you will realize that you aren't enjoying your feelings. Shrugging off responsibility only increases guilt. The more you give in to your feelings, the worse you will feel. Rather than knowing fulfillment, you will feel restless and dissatisfied.

A man may be depressed because he is unable to finish his work around the house. He hopes that someday he will feel like taking out the garbage, trimming the hedges, washing the cars, and fixing the fence. But right now he doesn't feel like it. Furthermore, even if he were to begin today, there would still be more work tomorrow. So instead, he follows his feelings and lies on the sofa to watch TV. Because he is doing what he feels like doing, he should be happy and satisfied, right?

Wrong! Guilt settles upon him like a London fog. Each day the work he should be doing piles up higher and higher. His children and his spouse begin to complain. Because he has fallen so far behind, he feels as though there is no use in trying to catch up. Through it all, his frustration will never leave until he chooses to do what he ought—whether he feels like it or not.

The moment you declare war on your besetting sin, you will bump into your feelings, mostly unhelpful ones. Be prepared for a feeling of helplessness, the feeling that you are a victim of circumstances you cannot change and desires you cannot control. These feelings just happen to be the sin of unbelief in a different form. They are one of the tools Satan uses to get you to believe that either God cannot or will not help you.

Very soon, discouragement will pry its way into your life. It usually hits a few days after you've decided to make a clean break with sin and develop habits of righteousness. Satan's line goes something like this: "You've tried to break this habit and failed. There is no reason to try again. You're not good enough for God to want to help you."

Another feeling you may have to battle is laziness—the notion that you need not put too much effort into the Christian life. You'll be tempted to procrastinate, to put off any serious attempt at seeking God's will concerning your problem. Satan never fears your good intentions. Only your obedience drives him to distraction.

Now take a hard look at your feelings and then ask yourself: "How can I cope with them?"

Look to Christ's Example

Jesus Christ, as a man, experienced every human emotion. He wept at the grave of Lazarus. As He faced the indescribable assignment of bearing the sin of the world, He was traumatized by an excruciating emotional burden. Yet Jesus did not spend those last hours in self-pity, bemoaning His fate. He handled the experience constructively, and therefore provided a model for us all. What did He do?

First, He admitted His feelings: "My soul is overwhelmed with sorrow to the point of death. Stay here and keep watch with me" (Matthew 26:38). He allowed His disciples to have a glimpse of the unutterable passions that came upon Him in the dark. Suppressing your feelings will not cause them to disappear. Feelings must be dealt with honestly; they should not be ignored. Needless to say, Jesus' emotional upheavals did not lead Him to sinful thoughts or behavior, but even so, you must follow Him by honestly acknowledging how you feel. Admitting your bitterness, depression, hatred, or passion is the first step in learning to cope with your feelings.

We've all met people who will not admit to their feelings. A pastor once told of a deacon who, with a clenched fist and a flushed face, pounded on the table and shouted, "I'm not angry!" A woman who recited in meticulous detail all the wrongs her husband had committed against her ended her indictment with the startling statement, "Of course I'm not bitter; I've forgiven him for these things." But her careful cataloging of all the wrongs he had done betrayed her. Think of how often we are unwilling to admit how we really feel!

David, the psalmist, was vulnerably honest. Read his psalms, and you will be struck by the wide range of emotions that he felt. When he was joyful, he shouted praises; when he was depressed, he complained about God's silence and apparent indifference to his need. Depression, joy, and even anger were freely admitted. We don't know how often David told others about his woes, but we know he spent much time giving his problems to God. The first step, then, is to admit the truth about your emotions and tell God how you feel.

Second, Jesus requested the support of friends. He had three groups of disciples: the seventy, who went from house to house to proclaim the kingdom; the twelve, who were constantly with Him; and the three within that circle who were given special opportunities. Peter, James, and John, who had been invited to the Mount of Transfiguration, were asked to help their Master bear intense suffering. Jesus did not consider it beneath His dignity to ask His friends for prayerful intercession and companionship in the hour of trial.

Personally, I believe that many so-called emotional problems could be solved by corporate intercessory prayer. But the church today is much like the disciples who found praying more difficult than sleeping. Their spirit was willing, but their flesh was weak.

Third, Jesus knew that His emotional suffering would not separate Him from the Father's love and approval. Their relationship was not affected by the weight of His anguish. As believers we need to realize that our acceptance before God is unrelated to our feelings. We do not live the Christian life by moods, but by faith. Freedom comes to us when we understand that our walk with God is not dependent on how we feel when we get out of bed in the morning.

Finally, Jesus knew that blessing would follow obedience. Emotional peace and calm would come after doing God's will and not before. The assurance of joy in the future enabled Him to endure the tortures of the present. The author of Hebrews inspires us with the example of Jesus, telling us that as we pursue victory over the "sin that so easily entangles [us]" (Hebrews 12:1), we can fix our "eyes on Jesus, the pioneer and perfecter of faith. For the joy set before him he endured the cross, scorning its shame, and sat down at the right hand of the throne of God" (verse 2).

Remember that feelings flow from action, and not vice versa. You can prove this fact tomorrow morning. If you follow your feelings, you will not get out of bed when the alarm clock rings. If you wait for the proper feeling, your day will begin behind schedule. But if you choose to get up and start getting ready to go to work, whether you feel like it or not, you will soon discover that you are feeling pretty good. And by the time you have finished your breakfast, you will be thinking that life isn't so bad after all. Proper feelings come because of action; they do not precede the action itself.

✶Whenever we obey God, our feelings begin to fall in line. We have a sense of satisfaction, a sense of self-esteem. Feelings follow faith and obedience. So don't wait for that magic moment when you feel like obeying, feel like committing yourself to God, or feel like praying and reading your Bible. ✶

We all have tasks we dislike doing. What makes us think we should wait until we feel like doing them? Jesus did not feel like dying on the cross. He suffered more physical pain than we can ever comprehend, along with excruciating moral anguish. Imagine what the sinless One endured as He became identified with the sin of the world. Every emotional conflict known to man (except personal guilt) convulsed within the body of the Son of God. But He went ahead with God's will because He was obedient unto death, even death upon a cross (Philippians 2:8). Why did He do it? Jesus knew that after obedience there is joy. How often we have reversed the order. We think we've got to be in the right mood to obey God. But there is no joy until there is obedience.

One final word: We must learn to give thanks to God for all things, whether we feel like it or not. The focus of our attention must be the truth that is settled in heaven. Several years ago, I experienced a short period of depression. I learned in a matter of hours that depression is real; it's not just a fantasy. The evening it hit, life seemed useless. The phrase that kept popping into my head was, "Vanity of vanities, all is vanity" (Ecclesiastes 1:2 NKJV). I had always told others that the cure for depression was praise. It was time for me to take a dose of my own medicine.

Months before this incident, I had prepared a list of all the blessings that God has given us in Christ. Resisting all my negative emotional impulses, I began to thank God for each one. Even though I didn't feel thankful, I was grateful mentally, and I told God so. Even reciting the verses of Scripture and giving thanks seemed to be futile. Yet I continued, resisting the thought of quitting. It wasn't long before the depression left. Of course, I'm not suggesting that all depression can be handled so simply. But when it comes to tackling our emotional moods, praise is the place to begin.

I've discovered a new liberty in my Christian life since realizing that my faith need not be tied to my feelings. We honor God when we walk by faith without emotional supports. And within time, our feelings will catch up with the truth that we accept with our minds. In practical terms, this means that you can begin right now to take constructive steps toward positive change. You'll never feel more like doing it than at this very moment. The action step and questions at the end of this chapter will help you to get started right now.

ACTION STEP: What do you dislike doing, yet know that you *should* do? Every day, determine to do one thing you dislike doing. It may be as simple as cleaning your desk or as difficult as asking the forgiveness of someone you have wronged. Learn to not be controlled by your feelings, but by what you should and can do by the power of the Holy Spirit.

Questions for Personal Reflection or Small Group Study

1. What evidence is there that many people today emphasize physical comfort (feelings and pleasure) rather than a life of self-denial? Earlier in the chapter it was said that most sinful habits are developed because we prefer to follow the path of least resistance. Do you see evidence of this in your own life? In what areas? What can you do now to begin heading in another direction?

2. A friend of mine, Henry Teichrob, used to say this:

   > Faith often runs counter to feeling. Even the attempt to find victory in feelings is a sin in the life of a believer. In short, it is simply "walking in the flesh." We must repent of the sin of assessing the reality of the Christ-life on the basis of feeling.

   Discuss the above statement with questions such as these in mind: Why do our feelings fluctuate? Why do we so often think that spirituality is to be equated with "feeling just right"? Find some examples in Scripture where faith runs contrary to feelings. What can we learn from those examples?

3. Read the words of Jesus in John 12:27-28. What was the outcome of the struggle between Jesus' feelings and His determination to do God's will? What duties do you have that you do not feel like doing? Why, then, do you do those things? What would happen if you only did whatever you felt like doing?

4. The chapter lists a series of steps you can take to overcome your feelings about a certain task or obstacle: First, you must admit your feelings. Second, you must ask for help from your friends and from God. Third, you must realize that your relationship with God is not dependent upon emotions—either yours or His. Finally, you must realize that blessing follows obedience. Spend some time now in prayer practicing these steps with regard to the stubborn habit you're trying to overcome.

5. What practical benefits are there in realizing that we walk by faith and not by emotional sight? Write a list of blessings that God has given you in Christ. Take some time now to thank the Lord for these blessings, and make it a habit to do so often.

CHAPTER 9

The Taming of Your Will

Ultimately, we are controlled by our greatest desires.

just don't have any willpower!"

We've all said those words, whether we were trying to lose weight, live by a budget, or fight an addiction. How frustrating to know what we ought to do, and yet not have the strength to do it! The gap between knowledge and performance is often embarrassing. We just can't seem to get ourselves moving in the right direction. Yet unless we can use our will effectively, we will always default to the same old habits and fall back into the same old behavioral ruts.

Can your will be disciplined? Yes. You do not need to drift aimlessly through life, carried along like a cork on a river. You can learn to make responsible decisions and say no to the path of least resistance. The key is this: *to develop your desire to please God more than your desire to please yourself.*

What Is Your Will?

You might be wondering what your "will" is. Your will is your decision-making faculty. Often it is caught between your thoughts and your desires. Your emotions express how you feel, your mind says what you know, but your will decides the direction you will go. The weary disciples experienced this tension in Gethsemane. Jesus asked them twice to watch and pray with Him, but both times they fell asleep. Our Savior commented, "Watch and pray so that you will not fall into temptation. The spirit is willing, but the flesh is weak" (Matthew 26:41).

Now let's bring this subject a little closer to home—to your own bedroom, for instance. The alarm rings at 6:00 a.m., and your mind knows full well what that means: You should carefully move from a horizontal to a vertical position. But your body feels differently about the matter. Now your will has to make a decision that cannot satisfy both the body and the mind. And your will has only a few moments to decide to do so, or you will drift into unconscious comfort for another hour.

What determines whether your will follows the direction of the mind or the inclinations of the body? It depends on your desires and your determination to fulfill such desires. If your job is important to you, you'll be strongly inclined to get out of bed. If your temporary comfort is more attractive than a paycheck, you'll tend to ignore the alarm clock.

If you were born into a home with little discipline and weak commitment to dependability, you'll have a strong tendency to do whatever comes naturally. However, background cannot be used as an excuse for laziness, because those who were reared in well-disciplined homes fight the same natural desires. Believe it or not, we are all much the same inside!

Heredity also influences the will. We've all inherited tendencies from the temperaments of our parents. Those who have studied human nature believe they have discovered several distinct patterns. There are some things about us that will never change. To use a computer illustration: Our hardware never changes, but we can make changes to our software. Our basic traits may never change, but our attitude and behavior can be changed with God's help.

Think of what we have to overcome! Romans 3:10-11 reads, "There is no one righteous, not even one; there is no one who understands; there is no one who seeks God." Left to ourselves, we would never seek God. He comes seeking us and changing our desires so that we might be better able to live up to what we know to be right and good.

Jesus taught that no one can come to Him unless drawn by the Father (John 6:44-65). God does not save us by circumventing our will. He works through our will, giving us the ability to choose to believe in Christ and also to do what is right. You have heard the expression, "Let go and let God," which implies that God will take over and control us completely if we wish Him to do so. But this is not the teaching of Scripture. Our will does not become passive when ✓ we yield to God. A surrendered will experiences struggle, as Jesus' conflict in Gethsemane demonstrates.

Fortunately, the Holy Spirit does not stop working with our will at the time of conversion. Paul wrote, "To this end I strenuously contend with all the energy Christ so powerfully works in me" (Colossians 1:29). The Holy Spirit stands ready to come to our aid the moment we face a temptation or a difficult decision.

The Basis of Choice

Before you can bring your will into harmony with God's purposes, you need the right goals for your life. If you don't believe that life is worth living, it won't make much difference to you whether you break sinful habits or reinforce them. A purposeful life, therefore, is the basis for discipline and determination to make right choices.

Day-to-day activities have short-term meaning. If you choose to clean the house, mow the lawn, or write a chapter of a book, you have a sense of satisfaction when the task is completed. Specific short-term goals give direction in how you use your time and can have long-term consequences. But temporary goals are not adequate for a meaningful and satisfying life. An insurance executive who had achieved all the short-term goals imaginable—two beautiful homes, several luxury cars, and plenty of vacation time—committed suicide because "life wasn't worth the trouble of living." He had reached all of his material goals and found that ultimately, they were not satisfying. Only eternal values can give meaning to temporal ones. Time must be the servant of eternity. Let's look at how this truth can be applied to your life.

First, take the example of Moses. Moses could say no to the world because he was firmly convinced that time (or eternity, if you please) would vindicate his choice. Focusing on the eternal gave him the resources to make wise choices on earth.

Given his values, Moses was willing to forego immediate pleasures. The Bible does not deny there is pleasure in short-term goals. In Pharaoh's court, Moses could have enjoyed wine, women, and song, as well as far-flung political power. But he knew that such pleasures are short-lived. He was able to postpone his immediate desires because of his faith in future rewards. He could say no to the world without thinking he had been shortchanged.

In Hebrews 11, the record of the faithful ones, we read,

> By faith, Moses, when he became of age, refused to be called the son of the Pharaoh's daughter, choosing rather to suffer affliction with the people of God than to enjoy the passing pleasures of sin, esteeming the reproach of Christ greater riches than the treasures in Egypt; for he looked to the reward. By faith he forsook Egypt, not fearing the wrath of the king; for he endured as seeing Him who is invisible (Hebrews 11:24-27 NKJV).

Moses endured temporary hardship because he saw the Invisible One. He saw the difference between time and eternity. Paul wanted the Corinthian Christians to "not look at the things which are seen, but at the things which are not seen. For the things which are seen are temporary, but the things which are not seen are eternal" (2 Corinthians 4:18 NKJV).

A mark of maturity is to accept the principle of delayed satisfaction, rather than the immaturity of the "now" generation that wants all of its kicks, thrills, and highs at this very moment. No consideration is given to tomorrow, much less the distant future. The permanent is sacrificed on the altar of the immediate.

Those who trust God can postpone fulfillment of their desires. Sex can wait until marriage; the discipline of hard study can be endured for the sake of an education; and any sinful pleasure can be abandoned in favor of the greater pleasure of fellowship with God. The question then is not whether we will have pleasure, but which pleasure we will have: the fleeting and ultimately unsatisfying pleasures of sin, or the lasting pleasures of God? We will follow whatever we love most.

Now let's look at the example of Jesus Christ. Jesus knew where He had come from, why He was here, and what He was supposed to accomplish. He came down from heaven not to do His own will, but the will of the Father. That determination controlled every decision He made. As a result, He was not distracted with the trivial. He was never in a hurry, for He knew His Father would not initiate a task without allotting the time to complete it. He was not driven by crises, feeling He had to heal everyone in Israel. He could say, "It is finished," even when many people were still bound by demons and twisted by disease. What mattered ultimately was not the number of people healed or fed, but whether the Father's will was being done. His clearly defined goals simplified His decisions.

We too need such a singleness of purpose. Dr. Ari Kiev of the Cornell Medical Center states, "Observing the lives of people who have mastered adversity, I have repeatedly noted that they have established goals and, irrespective of obstacles, sought with all their effort to achieve them. From the moment they've fixed an objective in their mind and decide to concentrate all their energies on a specific goal, they begin to surmount the most difficult odds."[5]

✳ This means we must stop putting first-rate value on third-rate priorities. We need to establish once and for all that our goal is to please our Father in heaven. Once we repent of our idolatries and know that God is our goal, it is much easier to make the right decisions. Indeed, the journey becomes a pleasure. ✳ *We must develop a passion for Christ that is greater than our passion to sin.*

How Do We Set Goals?

The invisible is more valuable than the visible. The eternal is more enduring than the temporal. But what do these facts have to do with our values, our goals? Our goals are set on the foundation of our larger beliefs about life and about ourselves. It is within the framework of our ultimate commitments that we formulate our short-range goals.

Let me suggest three levels of commitment that are appropriate for the Christian: (1) a commitment to God in Christ, (2) a commitment to the body of Christ, and (3) a commitment to the work God has given us to do. These three levels are the outline by which you can specify what you want to accomplish with your life. It is your responsibility to creatively spell out how you plan to fulfill these goals. For example, your commitment to God might mean that you spend half an hour each day getting to know the One to whom you have committed yourself. You may want to cut the amount of time you spend watching TV, or even cancel your cable subscription.

You will want to set goals in other parts of your life too.

You may want to lose some excess pounds. A body redeemed by God should be healthy. Once you decide how much weight you plan to lose and the diet you will follow, stay with it! Choose to forego immediate desires. When you are tempted by foods that are not part of your diet, remind yourself that this immediate pleasure can be postponed. Your goal to honor God should mean more to you than the craving for excess food. But be careful that such a diet—or any other commitment—does not become a god unto itself. God desires a healthy balance for our lives.

Of course, the value of such discipline will reach into such everyday activities as getting out of bed in the morning, carrying out the garbage, or washing windows. You can bring your body under control and do what is in line with the person you hope to become. If you value your commitments to God, then make sure that your yes and your no are consistent with your long-term goals.

Your momentary feelings are not a good guide toward fulfilling desirable goals. Paul had his body in control: "I strike a blow to my body and make it my slave so that after I have preached to others, I myself will not be disqualified for the prize" (1 Corinthians 9:27). You simply cannot give in to all the desires of your body. You would reap severe consequences if you did!

Surrendering to God Is Difficult

It is good to set priorities, to have goals. But what about your "want-to"? Your will? How are you going to hold to these goals you are setting that fit into your belief about God's desire for your life?

Setting good goals is not easy. And staying with them is even harder. As a Christian, you need the help of God as you seek to do His will. And yet it is just at this point that conflict arises.

> The struggle between our own selfish will and God's will is intense. We've learned that we were born with the desire to control our own destinies, to do our own thing. Consequently, our fallen will is adept at making choices in harmony with our pride, independence, and self-determination. We resist the idea that God should rule over us, particularly when it comes to our private affairs.

Perhaps you don't want God to decide whether or not you have a marriage partner. You don't want to submit your plans to a higher authority for approval. If you want to spend your Sunday afternoon watching football, that ought to be your decision. Or if you are skimpy in giving your money to the local church, that is your business. Entrusting yourself wholly to God seems rather impractical. If you don't take care of yourself, who will? You have to look out for ol' number one!

> It is just this kind of attitude that shows the need to learn obedience and humility. Usually we think that the human will must be strengthened, but paradoxically we become stronger only when we become weaker. When we surrender our will to God, we finally discover the resources to do what God requires. As we give ourselves to Him, trusting His promises, we receive His power.

When we are at the end of our rope, God is there to catch us—but not before. David knew that the most he could offer God was a yielded will: "The sacrifices of God are a broken spirit, a broken and a contrite heart—these, O God, You will not despise" (Psalm 51:17 NKJV). Submission to God always involves humility; it is an acknowledgment that we are neither qualified nor able to do what we ought to do. The temptation to strive with the Almighty is ever with us.

A businessman woke up early one Sunday morning and went golfing with some friends. He knew there was a men's meeting at the church, part of a revival that was in progress. When he finished playing 18 holes, it was noon. His curiosity made him stop at the church on his way home. He hoped the meeting would be over. But if not, he would at least "check to see who was there." To his amazement, half of the men were on their knees, many of them weeping. Others had left the room for special prayer. He let all of this spiritual activity register for a moment and then angrily clenched his fist and slammed it into his other hand, and said, "You'll never get me, God!"

Get him for what? What would make a Christian say such a thing? The matter most pressing on his mind was his relationship with his children. The man was victimized by a hot temper, and many times he had hurt his children's feelings and wounded their spirits. He knew that if God "got" him, he would have to humble himself and ask the forgiveness of his children. He decided that the price was too great.

When we fight against the demands of God, trying to weasel out of whatever doesn't suit us, our will is pitted against His in a desperate struggle for survival. But when we say yes to God, we discover the ability to do His will. Strength is dependent upon surrender.

God did "get" the businessman. He humbled himself and went to his children to ask their forgiveness. Later, as he told how God had broken him, he wept unashamedly. God gave him the willpower to do what he could not do on his own. And his will was energized by the Holy Spirit when he stopped resisting and chose to say no to his sin. At that point it became possible for God to work through the man's will to accomplish His purpose.

You Can Manage the Conflict

Does temptation ever lose its power? Not completely. Even when we are motivated by a desire to please God, we experience conflict because God often requires obedience that runs counter to human motivations. Jesus Himself expressed this conflict: "I have come down from heaven, not to do My own will, but the will of Him who sent Me" (John 6:38 NKJV). He voluntarily set aside any personal ambitions and submitted Himself to His Father's will.

The conflicts between your immediate interests and God's long-range goals are never going to go away. But there is an answer. When you begin to commit yourself to God, the Holy Spirit helps to resolve these conflicts. He pulls the fragments of your life together. He shows you His truth as a standard for making choices. He teaches you a single-mindedness that you never knew before. He shows you the rewards of living in His love and justice. And after a while, you begin to realize that in many instances, what God requires of you is really what you want to do. Just as the psalmist wrote: "Take delight in the LORD, and he will give you the desires of your heart" (Psalm 37:4).

This helps us understand Jesus' conflict. True, His human inclinations ran contrary to what the Father's will required. Paul said that Jesus did not please Himself (Romans 15:3). But His satisfaction in doing God's will was much greater than the natural desire to avoid suffering. The prophet predicted that Christ would say, "I desire to do your will, my God" (Psalm 40:8).

Visualize a piece of steel suspended between two magnets. It vacillates, swinging from the right to the left or vice versa. For a moment it wavers. It could go either way because it is being simultaneously drawn in opposing directions by two powerful forces. After wavering for a second, it begins to move in one direction or the other. Then it moves more rapidly, unable to swing back anymore. It is out of the range of the other magnet's power.

You may be hovering between God and the world. Sometimes you follow your own desires, sometimes God's. No one knows what your eventual decision will be. But the farther you go in God's direction, the less attraction the world will have. The day will come when your choices will be easier. Saying yes to God can be habit-forming.

There is another lesson you can learn from this illustration. You can't say no to temptation unless you say yes to God. Like the magnet, the world will never lose its power to attract. To merely resist its power is pointless; no will is strong enough. But if you focus your attention on God as revealed in the Scriptures, you remove yourself from the sphere of the world's influence.

I have found that I can't resist enticing thoughts simply by saying, "I resist that thought!" The thought returns again and again. I do, however, have the ability to switch my thoughts to the Scriptures—quote a verse, offer praise, or renew my fellowship with God. Only in the presence of the Almighty does the world lose its allure.

God has given us the resources to say no to sin. Paul urged his readers to obey, but not merely by appealing to their unaided human wills. He reminded them that "it is God who works in you to will and to act in order to fulfill his good purpose" (Philippians 2:13). God works in us by energizing our will. He helps us make the decisions that we ought to make, and ultimately really want to make.

God uses our struggles with temptation to teach us how to depend on His power. The ninth fruit of the Spirit is self-control (Galatians 5:23). That word, *self-control,* means literally "to hold oneself in." It refers to the mastery of desires—in the interest of higher ideals.

Don't feel powerless against a barrage of temptations. Maybe you have an insatiable desire for drugs, alcohol, or sex. Maybe your sins are restricted to your mind. Whatever your sins, there is hope. Like Jesus, Moses, and an innumerable host of saints before you, you can eventually say no to any stubborn habit by setting the right priorities. And the more you learn to love Christ, the less you will be attracted by the world. Remember, it is always more important to please Christ than it is to please ourselves!

ACTION STEP: Read Romans 7:14-25, and see how clearly Paul describes his own dilemma in trying to bring his will in line with God. Then read Romans 8 and absorb the optimism he experiences once he reminds himself of the power of the Spirit and the blessings given to all those who trust in Christ.

1. Read Psalm 73, written by Asaph, who was wondering whether serving God was worthwhile. Notice particularly how his problem was solved when he began to focus on eternal rather than temporal rewards. What temporal things in your own life could you do with a little less of in order to embrace a little more eternity? Write them down.

2. Ponder Proverbs 25:28. Describe the characteristics of someone who has no control over his spirit. What are the advantages of being disciplined?

3. Take an inventory of your life by asking yourself: In what areas am I resisting God's complete ownership? Suggested areas might be your schedule, pleasures, recreation, vocation, health, reputation, marital status, friendships, computer time, to name a few. Pray right now and give these areas fully to God.

4. Take some time now to make a list of your short- and long-term goals according to the levels of commitment laid out earlier in the chapter: (1) a commitment to God in Christ, (2) a commitment to the body of Christ, and (3) a commitment to the work God has given you to do.

5. If you have not already done so, set aside 20 minutes each morning to begin the day with God. You'll be tempted not to follow through with this commitment. Write down what those temptations might be, and prepare yourself by developing a strategy to combat those temptations.

CHAPTER 10

The Intercession of Christ and Believers

Get others to pray for you, and know that
Someone very powerful is already praying for you.

I'm sometimes reminded of a horse we had on our farm growing up. One day he walked into a slough on his own, and we had to pull him out with a tractor.

Just like that horse, it is possible for us to develop the worst habits on our own, and then need help getting out of the behavioral ruts. We fall into sin quite easily, and cannot get out on our own.

One summer day, I ate lunch with a man who has been helping men say no to Internet pornography. I was expecting him to give me some new spiritual truth I had not previously known so I could pass it on to those who struggle. To my surprise, he said the most helpful piece of advice for men is to join a small group of other men for Bible study and prayer. Through interpersonal relationships and accountability, God honors the humility and faithfulness of those who stand together in overcoming temptations and sins.

The body of Christ is not just powerful to help its members overcome stubborn habits. It also can help those who are experiencing spiritual defeat of any kind—depression, for instance.

Susan was planning to die on August 22. She had been a believer for 12 years and had no doubt that she was God's child. She taught Sunday school, witnessed, and tried to live "a good Christian life."

But she was still experiencing prolonged periods of depression. Her health was failing, and pressures in the home had become unbearable. Two of her older children were rebellious, and Susan couldn't cope with it all. She had looked to her husband for support and felt that he was insensitive and cold; he just didn't understand what she was going through. She read books to find an answer, but nothing seemed to help. Her only relief was through tranquilizers and sleeping pills. She felt she was alone in the struggle and no one else could help her.

Her next step was to contemplate divorce. She recalls, "I wanted out—fast." Her husband had recently committed himself to Christ at a meeting in their home church. Susan was glad; he needed it. But now she began to think her husband didn't love her anymore. He just walked around with a smile on his face, completely relaxed, and seemed more insensitive than ever.

Susan had had enough of everything, including life itself. She awoke on August 22 and meticulously planned her last day on earth: She would help her 16-year-old son get his driving permit, and perhaps even straighten out a few things in the house. Her sleeping pills were with her. She was at peace, confident she had made the right decision.

When she arrived back home with her son, she went to change her clothes. "Where are you going?" her son asked. "To the ladies' meeting at the church," she answered thoughtlessly. "Do you have to?" he responded. Susan did not want to go, but decided that she would. Unusual events had been going on at the church; in fact, a revival was in progress. The ladies were having a special meeting. Still confident that this would be her last day on earth, she cried the four miles to the church. "Lord," she prayed, "I know John will be better off with a new wife; the children will be better off with a different mother."

Trembling, she entered the sanctuary. The smiles on the women's faces only amplified her own depression. She did not participate in the singing. Instead, she wept for 15 minutes.

When the group stopped for lunch, she would not eat. She had been without food for four days and didn't plan to eat now. A woman invited her to come to the prayer room for some counsel and prayer. Susan's struggle was intense. She had not planned on confessing her sins and yielding herself to God. But four other women joined her; they read the Scriptures with her and then they began to pray. There on their knees, the women interceded for Susan. An hour passed before the long ordeal was over. When Susan emerged from the prayer room, she recalls that she "had no thought of death. I had never felt so alive in all my life."

Six months later she wrote, "Even though Satan has buffeted me a number of times, I can say that God does all things well, because truly His power is shown in weakness. I do have a health problem— but the depression is gone."

Susan's experience illustrates an important biblical principle: We cannot successfully live the Christian life on our own. God never intended that any one of us experience either failure or success alone, independent of the body of Christ. We need God's people for encouragement and intercession, and for the strength that comes from close fellowship.

And perhaps more important, we need the intercession of Christ. Our sin is never a private matter. We cannot say, "It only hurts me." God, Christ, and Satan are all involved in our failures, whether public or private. Satan accuses us before the Father, the Son intercedes for us, and the Father gives the verdict. Lewis Sperry Chafer used to say of sin, "It may be a secret on earth; but it is open scandal in heaven." [6]

The Intercession of Christ

Whenever tragedy strikes a family, the people who can be of most comfort are those who have had a similar experience. A widow can be of comfort to another widow; bereaved parents are helped by the support of others who have lost a child. There are two reasons. First, it's encouraging to know that others have survived a similar difficulty. Second, all of us want to meet someone who knows how we feel.

Christ qualifies on both counts. He experienced every temptation we've ever encountered. He was assaulted by Satan and hounded
by physical distress. He faced hunger, rejection, and death successfully. And today, He is deeply moved by our own feelings and struggles. The excruciating pain of the cross, coupled with the horror of
being identified with sin, was more torment than we could ever bear.
That's why the Scriptures can say, "We do not have a high priest who
is unable to empathize with our weaknesses, but we have one who
has been tempted in every way, just as we are—yet he did not sin"
(Hebrews 4:15).

Today, Jesus says to us, "I know how you feel." Furthermore, He
is moved with compassion—sympathy, if you please—for our weaknesses. Can we confront Satan and win? Can we experience death
and arrive safely on the other side? Jesus did, and in Him, we can too!
Because He endured His temptations, He offers all of us hope. Today
He is at the right hand of God the Father, making intercession for us
(Romans 8:34). His presence reminds the Father that we have been
bought at a high cost. When we sin, He takes up our case and assumes
all of the legal aspects of our relationship with God (1 John 2:1).

An example of His power of intercession is seen in the life of
Simon Peter. After the Lord's Supper was instituted, Jesus said to him,
"Simon, Simon, Satan has asked to sift all of you as wheat. But I have
prayed for you, Simon, that your faith may not fail. And when you
have turned back, strengthen your brothers" (Luke 22:31-32).

Peter retorted, "Lord, I am ready to go with you to prison and to
death" (verse 33). Jesus was not impressed. He knew that hours later,
Peter would deny Him as his courage turned to cowardice.

Was Jesus' prayer answered? Yes! Peter did deny Him, but the story
doesn't end there. It says, "He went outside and wept bitterly" (verse
62). After Peter repented, he was able to comfort and strengthen others. His ministry, as recorded in the book of Acts and in his letters
to the young and suffering church, are proof that Jesus' prayer was
answered.

Satan sifted Peter and discovered that he was part chaff and part wheat. But because of the intercession of Jesus, the chaff was blown away, and the wheat became nourishment for others in need. God gives Satan permission to do the same to us. Temptation, struggles, and failures are all part of the process. Most of us, like Peter, are a mixture of chaff and wheat, as our track record shows. But our Lord is qualified to keep us from stumbling irrevocably. "Because he himself suffered when he was tempted, he is able to help those who are being tempted" (Hebrews 2:18).

What an encouragement! Think again about that sin in your life that you can't seem to conquer. The outcome of that struggle is intensely important to God. It's a contest between Christ and Satan, and you happen to be the trophy!

But Christ is not the only one who intercedes for us. He invites all believers to participate in this rewarding ministry. Remember Jesus' intercession in Gethsemane? He was struggling with the prospect of the cross and asked His disciples to watch with Him. Three times He asked them to participate in His agony. They failed because they were too weary, but the invitation was there. Christ gives us the same opportunity. We can intercede with Him on behalf of other believers. We're invited to join Him in a ministry of intercession.

The Intercession of Believers

Sometimes our besetting sin won't budge until we enlist the prayer support of God's people, particularly in the case of addiction to alcohol, drugs, or sexual misconduct. We need the added support of others who will stand for us in the presence of God. Recently, after I had spoken at a church meeting, a young woman struggling with homosexual behavior came up to talk to me. She was feeling morally weak; in fact, she wasn't even sure she wanted to change her lifestyle. Clearly, she needed the persistent prayers and encouragement of God's people to help her come to terms with her problem.

Why is this necessary? Why doesn't an all-powerful God just give us victory if we individually apply the right principles? On the surface, it seems odd that our failure or success should be determined by other believers' faithfulness or negligence. Why the need for others to become involved in our personal affairs?

Primarily, it is because God wants us to give up our independent spirit. By nature, we are creatures who prefer to live according to our own blueprint. How we live is our business—what right does anyone have to ask or even be interested in how we are progressing spiritually? If we want them to know, we'll tell them!

The New Testament teaches otherwise. We are all members of the body of Christ, and each of us affects the function of others. If you have ever had a toothache, you know that the parts of your body are not isolated. When a tooth aches, your whole body hurts.

Have you ever seen a human hand severed from a body? It looks gruesome. Yet attached to an arm and connected to the nervous system, the hand is not only highly useful, but beautiful, too. The difference lies in its relationship to the body. Similarly, in Christ, no individual is anything if cut off from the body.

That's why God wants us to enlist the resources of other believers. It's humbling to realize that we need their support and help, but we do. Our struggles and temptations remind us that successes or failures are always a team effort. There's no room in the body of Christ for an individual scorecard. And the pride that keeps us from being honest with one another has to be broken.

That's why we must be acquainted with God's people. We must form friendships in church, where committed believers gather for fellowship and instruction. Within the larger circle of believers, we'll find that some will become special friends. As we develop confidence in them, we can turn to them in our time of need. At that moment, we are tapping a reservoir of spiritual power. Jesus said, "Where two or three gather in my name, there am I with them" (Matthew 18:20). The first responsibility of God's people is persistent prayer for one another; not merely individual prayer, but corporate prayer. Prayer as a group is important.

Recently I talked to a couple who was deeply hurt because a child they had adopted was taken away from them by the child's natural mother. Hopelessly neurotic and bitter, the biological mother had found her son and kidnapped him. Understandably, this Christian couple, who had accepted this boy from birth, was deeply upset. "Everyone is praying for us, but there's been no break in the case," the distraught woman told me. When I asked if people met with them for prayer, she responded, "No, but they all say they are praying for us." My suggestion to her was that they select a group of people, perhaps six, to meet with them regularly for prayer. It's not enough for people to say, "We're praying." There is supportive value in sharing our heartbreaks with a group of God's people. Jesus, you will recall, wanted the disciples to be at His side during His agony in Gethsemane. It wasn't only their prayers that He wanted. He wanted companionship during those agonizing moments, to give and receive encouragement.

A second way others can help is by keeping us responsible and accountable. We can agree to report to a group, or at least to one individual, on spiritual progress. If I know someone is going to ask me, "How's that problem coming?" I'm going to be more inclined to flee from temptation. One man suggested to his friend, "Whenever you are tempted to take another drink, call my cell phone, any time of day, and we'll pray together."

When I was in seminary, a close friend of mine and I met together for sharing and prayer every Thursday evening at 9:30. We were able to be honest with each other and give reports on our failures and successes. Knowing about that appointment was an incentive for me to keep watch on my actions so that I would not let my friend down. Of course, when we do fail, we need to be honest. Our pride will urge us to say that all is well when it is not. But when we develop responsibility toward others, it helps us do what we ought.

This practice of checking on each other can be used in many different ways. Some time ago another friend of mine and I agreed to learn the essential teaching of one chapter of the Bible every day. Occasionally we called each other on the telephone just to check on how we were doing. "What's in chapter 12?" he would ask, and that meant I had to know the answer cold. When I was tempted to let the project slide, I reminded myself of that commitment and how I would feel if I were to fail his quiz.

A man who struggled with homosexuality once told me that he would not go downtown without the companionship of another Christian. The man simply did not trust himself. The temptation to cruise and slide back into his former ways was too strong. But with a Christian companion along, he would not succumb to such enticement. Later, when he became stronger spiritually, he did not need such support.

God wants to teach us that we cannot live a successful Christian life independent of His children. If we are wayward, we must be restored; if we are weak, others must share their strength with us. At no time should we begin to think that we can make it alone with God, for we need His redeemed people too.

Restoring a Believer

What should we do when we see a fellow believer trapped in a sinful habit? Discuss the matter with our friends? Or do nothing, hoping that someday he or she will snap out of it?

The Bible is explicit about our responsibility. If a believer has erred, and not merely violated certain personal preferences, it is our responsibility to restore him or her, and bring the person to a right relationship with God. Jesus instructed,

> If your brother or sister sins, go and point out their fault, just between the two of you. If they listen to you, you have won them over. But if they will not listen, take one or two others along, so that "every matter may be established by the testimony of two or three witnesses." If they still refuse to listen, tell it to the church; and if they refuse to listen even to the church, treat them as you would a pagan or a tax collector (Matthew 18:15-17).

Our first responsibility is to go to that individual in private. We shouldn't tell our friends, our relatives, or even our pastor! At this point, there is no reason to make the sin public. If the brother or sister is repentant and is given instruction on how to break from their sin, there is no reason for others to become involved.

We've all disobeyed God on this score. Confronting another believer in love takes courage, so we prefer the cowardly route of gossip. We pass the news to others, thinking they should help, or at least "pray." Baser motives often lie beneath such excuses. We delight in other people's faults because that gives us an exalted feeling of superiority. "I'd never do that," we say.

Churches split and family relationships are shattered beyond repair because believers do not have the courage to go to a fellow Christian caught in a sin. Matters that should be cared for in private mushroom into bitter confrontations when people choose sides on the issues. Such is the price of cowardice. More accurately, such is the fruit of disobedience.

Paul gave some instructions regarding our attitude in the restoration process. If the person's sin is generally known, the church should select qualified members to confront the believer in love. "Brothers and sisters, if someone is caught in a sin, you who live by the Spirit should restore that person gently. But watch yourselves, or you also may be tempted" (Galatians 6:1). We've already mentioned that sin in another person's life tends to generate self-righteousness in us. We like to feel superior and believe we are immune to similar temptation. That type of an attitude will stifle any attempt to restore a fellow believer. Paul warns that we dare not come across as super-Christians. We must go in humility, knowing full well that we could slide into the same trespass.

Of course, the initial contact is not the end of the matter. We must be prepared to befriend, counsel, and pray with those who hurt. God wants every one of us to have a ministry in the life of another believer. I don't mean that this ministry must be one-sided; we'll soon discover that we cannot help others without being edified in return. We all need to be dependent on each other. Anything less fosters individualism—which, within the church, is sin.

Do you need help spiritually? Connect with other imperfect believers and become a mutual support system. God will most probably not let you break those stubborn habits on your own.

> **ACTION STEP:** Pray with someone today, even if it is just over the phone. Ask them to pray for you, and in return, take time to pray for them. You will find that God honors united prayer!

Questions for Personal Reflection and Group Study

1. Read 1 Corinthians 12. What responsibility does one member of the body of Christ have to another? Give specific examples. Why do you think that believers sometimes do not help each other as they ought?

2. Do you currently meet with anyone on a regular basis to discuss spiritual growth? What would such a relationship look like to you? If you haven't already, try to become a member of a small group of believers who pray together and support one another spiritually. Learn to share your concerns and struggles with them. Think of creative ways that the group could better help one another grow in Christ. Write down your thoughts.

3. In what ways have churches often given the impression that they are not interested in helping those with special needs? What can be done to change this impression—or fact?

4. How often do you clearly invite Christ to help you with your trials and temptations? The Bible tells us it is because of Christ we have access to the Father (John 16:23-27). So take some time right now to thank Jesus for what He did on the cross, and ask Him to guide you and give you wisdom as you deal with your struggles.

CHAPTER 11

Satanic Activity

The devil knows your weaknesses.

I enjoy watching *Animal Planet*. For example, I marvel at how lions hunt for food and have been created to survive in their environment. I've learned this about them: Lions do not roar when they are on the hunt—doing so would scare the prey away. Rather, they roar to mark territory and to keep their pride in line.

This trait is what Peter had in mind when he wrote, "Be alert and of sober mind. Your enemy the devil prowls around like a roaring lion looking for someone to devour. Resist him, standing firm in the faith" (1 Peter 5:8-9). The devil, or one of his many emissaries, tries to get us to think that we cannot be free of our habits and sins and wants to beat us into submission. He wants to say, "This area of your life is mine."

He has already made meticulous plans for our downfall. Behind the lies we want so desperately to believe is the Liar. He wants to run our behavioral ruts so deep that we can no longer say no to a habit, no matter how destructive it might be. Whether it's gambling, alcoholism, or a sexual addiction of some kind, our enemy wants to tighten the cords that bind us.

A casual look around us readily confirms that Americans are addicted to the media: the Internet, TV, movies, video games, cell phones, and other gadgets that can quickly lead to obsessive-compulsive behavior. It is all too easy for us to develop an insatiable appetite for these kinds of amusements—an appetite that can neither be satisfied nor changed. The media industry is Satan's playground. He uses it to distract us from what is really important as he attempts to turn us into robots who obey our appetites no matter how destructive they may be.

We must believe that satanic forces are involved in our spiritual struggles. Some Christians teach that the only time we confront satanic activity is in cases of bizarre behavior or dabbling in the occult. However, I believe that satanic powers can play a part in any sin that crops up in the routine of daily living. It's just that Satan prefers to work undercover.

Let's take lying as an example. Most Christians who tell an occasional lie would never suspect that Satan has anything to do with it. They may tell a "white lie" to wiggle out of an embarrassing circumstance or to protect their reputation. *Surely such behavior has no connection with Satan*, we think to ourselves. But consider the case of Ananias and Sapphira, which is recorded in Acts 5.

You'll recall they lied about the amount of money they received from the sale of their land. Let's assume they sold their land for $1,000, but when asked how much they got for it, they said $600. In one sense, they spoke the truth—they had sold it for $600, though they failed to say it was $600 plus $400! That is what some people would call a *trivial* white lie.

Who would have guessed that Satan was the instigator of this deception? When Peter confronted Ananias, he said, "How is it that Satan has so filled your heart that you have lied to the Holy Spirit and have kept for yourself some of the money you received for the land?" (Acts 5:3). Later, when Sapphira came by, Peter confronted her as well and said, "How could you conspire to test the Spirit of the Lord?" (verse 9). When Ananias and Sapphira had a discussion and agreed to tell a lie, they never realized that the devil had actually inserted that lie into their minds; they credited themselves with the idea.

Does Satan play a role in the breakup of a marriage? Paul warns that couples ought to meet one another's sexual needs "so that Satan will not tempt you because of your lack of self-control" (1 Corinthians 7:5). Again, Satan is there, doing whatever he can to ruin a marriage.

Let's suppose that your sin is cowardice. You just can't seem to open your mouth for Christ. You feel awkward and embarrassed to be identified with Him. Could these fears be instigated by the devil? When Peter denied Jesus, our Lord remarked that it was Satan who demanded that Peter be sifted as wheat (Luke 22:31). Yes, Satan was actively involved in Peter's denial of Christ. The evil one also hindered Paul from visiting the church at Thessalonica (1 Thessalonians 2:18). He is the originator of false doctrine, and the deceived are "taken captive by him to do his will" (2 Timothy 2:26 NKJV). Satan obscures the issues of the gospel and blinds the minds of the unsaved such that "they cannot see the light of the gospel that displays the glory of Christ, who is the image of God" (2 Corinthians 4:4). Also, Satan causes people to forget the Word of God by taking information out of their minds so that they will not be saved (Luke 8:12).

You may think you have never met a person who has had any contact with demonic forces. But you've met yourself, and I suspect that is sufficient. No one can escape contact with "the prince of the power of the air" (Ephesians 2:2 KJV), the one who has organized his army of wicked spirits to fight God's people.

Satan's Target

For centuries, philosophers and scientists have struggled with the problem of the nature of the mind. They have wrestled with questions such as, What are thoughts? What is the relationship between mind and body? But this much seems clear: Thoughts do not occupy space as we know it, but exist in a separate realm. For example, it would be absurd to speak of a thought as a quarter-inch long, or as occupying a specified area. Because thoughts exist in a spiritual realm, it's safe to say that the mind is vulnerable to spiritual influences as well.

The spiritual part of human beings exists in a realm that is not off-limits to spiritual forces, whether good or evil. We've already learned that it was the devil who gave Ananias and Sapphira the idea to lie about the sale of their land. Where do you think Judas got the idea to betray Jesus? John said that the devil put the suggestion into his heart (John 13:2). The mind is a target for satanic attack.

Satan loves exploiting our areas of weakness. He delights in influencing our passions, arousing our greed and anger, inflating our egos, and stirring up our hatred and resentment. All of this and more is done by the roaring lion who stalks the earth, "seeking whom he may devour" (1 Peter 5:8 KJV). We can be sure he is involved in our besetting sin.

Does his activity absolve us from any responsibility in committing sin? Not in the least. Peter did not let Ananias and Sapphira off the hook because their lie was instigated by Satan, and Judas was responsible for his betrayal of Jesus. If we allow satanic activity in our life, God will hold us responsible because we have the power to choose whether we will pursue Satan's suggestions. Yes, Satan might suggest that we lie, but the choice of whether to act on that suggestion is ours. He may tease us with any sin imaginable, but ultimately you and I make the choice. He cannot work independent of our cooperation.

Dealing with the Devil

Some Christians reason, "If I leave Satan alone, he'll leave me alone. I don't want to get involved." Without realizing it, these believers have unwittingly conceded the battle to the enemy. Satan has them exactly where he wants them, safely tucked away on the shelf labeled "Too Frightened to Fight." I tell such people, "You don't want to get involved? My friend, you are involved—you've just made peace with the enemy by refusing to do battle with him."

Satan's most successful weapon is fear. He will make you believe that if you take his existence seriously, he will create havoc in your home or ruin your peace of mind. Don't believe him. Satan "is a liar and the father of lies" (John 8:44). He will bluff you, push you as far as your ignorance will allow. But as a believer, you have the authority to renounce Satan's foothold in your life.

First, you must take inventory and check your armor. If there is one piece missing, you are vulnerable. That exposed area is exactly where the arrow will be aimed! Satan is an expert marksman. His arrows don't miss their target; you can't depend on a sloppy defense to get you by unscathed. This is one war in which good luck doesn't count.

In Ephesians 6:12-18, the apostle Paul presents the seven pieces of our spiritual armor as provided by God. In relation to what we are talking about here, let me comment on only one: the breastplate of righteousness. Satan always needs some reason to trouble us, some sin that gives him a right to our life. Once that sin is confessed and forsaken, his foothold disintegrates. He still will attack, but we need not fall for his enticements.

I've counseled people who feel uncomfortable when someone even mentions the blood of Jesus. Most often they will not even look me in the eye, but try to shy away. Usually it is because they have wandered into Satan's territory by refusing to deal thoroughly with their past sins.

It is righteousness that shields us from demonic attack. Satanic arrows are deflected when our conscience is void of offense. If you are finding yourself troubled by satanic attack, you should ask: Where have I given ground to Satan? What sins do I tolerate? Where do I resist God?

Personal righteousness, then, is essential in sealing yourself off from Satan's activity. But so are the other pieces of armor listed in Ephesians 6. They are numbered at the end of this chapter for your study.

Second, you need to realize that Satan has no rights, but won't admit it. Jesus' death and ascension effectively cut the ground from under him. Before His death, Jesus predicted, "Now is the time for judgment on this world; now the prince of this world will be driven out" (John 12:31). Jesus' death and ascension to heaven won a legal victory over all satanic forces—Jesus Christ beat Satan on his home turf. Paul wrote regarding Christ, "Having disarmed the powers and authorities, he made a public spectacle of them, triumphing over them by the cross" (Colossians 2:15). That's why James could write, "Submit yourselves, then, to God. Resist the devil, and he will flee from you" (4:7). Satan is allowed to maneuver through the atmosphere, causing havoc. But he can be successfully resisted. Paul wrote, "In your anger do not sin: Do not let the sun go down while you are still angry, and do not give the devil a foothold" (Ephesians 4:26-27).

Satan is like a dethroned king who keeps on giving orders to his subjects; he is like a thief who has stolen virtually everything you own and who tries to persuade you that it was always his. He is like a warrior without authority who keeps recruiting mercenaries to fight a battle he has already lost. You *can* say no to Satan!

Finally, remember that all believers have legal authority over demonic forces. There is a connection between Ephesians chapters 1 and 2 that is often overlooked. Near the end of the first chapter we read of God's great power, which was displayed in Christ:

> That power is the same as the mighty strength [God] exerted when he raised Christ from the dead and seated him at his right hand in the heavenly realms, far above all rule and authority, power and dominion, and every name that is invoked, not only in the present age but also in the one to come. And God placed all things under his feet and appointed him to be head over everything for the church, which is his body, the fullness of him who fills everything in every way (Ephesians 1:19-23).

I hope you read these verses carefully enough to see (1) that Christ's ascension to heaven placed Him above all rule, authority, power, "and every name that is named" (verse 21 KJV), and (2) that "all things [are] under His feet" (verse 22 NKJV). No power exists in the universe without Christ's permission.

And here is the good news that pulls it all together: In Ephesians 2:6, Paul says we are seated with Christ in heavenly places. This means that Satan and all of his wicked spirits are, at this very moment, under our feet!

Often we feel weak and helpless, but this does not diminish our position of authority. A policeman may not feel strong at all; indeed, he may be ill or exhausted. Physically, he would not be able to stop the smallest compact car; yet when he raises his hand, all the traffic stops. Why? Because the government has given him authority over traffic.

Some people have told me, "I hear voices that tell me to commit suicide. I'm afraid that one of these days I will do it." You and I need not listen to such voices! Satan likes to make people think that he can program them and that they must obey his commands. Christ's death and ascension have put an end to such lies. The message of the New Testament is clear: Christ won a complete victory over Satan, and believers can now participate in that triumph.

Demonic Activity and Our Sinful Habit

How do we confront wicked powers? Follow the example of Jesus, who commanded, "Away from me, Satan! For it is written..." (Matthew 4:10). You can claim the promises of Scripture to command Satan to depart. Earlier in this book we talked about the need for memorizing verses of Scripture that relate directly to specific temptations. Of course, simply shouting a verse of Scripture at demonic powers in and of itself does not make them cringe. In the temptation of Christ, Satan retorted with a verse of his own. The reason for citing Scripture is that the power of God's Word is unleashed when you bring yourself under its authority.

Although the disciples were given authority to expel demons, they discovered they were not always able to do so (Luke 9:1-6,37-43). At times they found themselves powerless because they had allowed the sin of unbelief to grow in their lives (Matthew 17:19-21). Furthermore, they were concerned about their own reputations and places in the kingdom of heaven. Jesus rebuked them for arguing about who would be the greatest among them (Luke 9:46-50). They were ineffective because their lives were no longer under God's authority.

God has given us the right to deal with demonic forces as long as we are under His authority. To put it simply, only those who are under authority can exercise authority. Satan and his forces must eventually back away when confronted by an obedient child of the living God who makes bold use of biblical truth. So don't be afraid to confront satanic forces directly when you are wrestling with sinister thoughts that refuse to leave.

Let me warn you that you may lose many battles, but eventually you will win the war. Slowly, your victories will begin to outnumber your defeats. You'll discover that you do have authority, just as the Scriptures teach. You will wrestle effectively against the kingdom of darkness and prove the Scripture that says, "He who is in you is greater than he who is in the world" (1 John 4:4 NKJV).

ACTION STEP: Below is a sample prayer you can lift up to God as you seek to take a stand against Satan:

Father, I thank You that Jesus Christ has ascended far above all principalities and powers. I rejoice that because I am joined to Him, I participate in His victory. I thank You that Satan and his armies have been defeated and must be subject to the exalted Savior. Now in Jesus' name, I ask that Satan's activity be stopped in my life [or, in the life of _____]. I bring the mighty truth of Christ's victory against all of Satan's workings. I desire to be in fellowship with You, the Son, and the Holy Spirit throughout this day. I offer this prayer to You, Father, in the name of the Lord Jesus Christ. Amen.

Questions for Personal Reflection and Group Study

1. If Satan wanted to destroy you, how would he do it? In what area of your life is he most likely to attack? What weakness makes you most vulnerable?

2. Here are the pieces of armor listed in Ephesians 6:12-18. Included is a brief description of what each piece ought to mean to you personally:

   a. The belt of truth (verse 14)—complete honesty.

   b. The breastplate of righteousness (verse 14)—confession of all sin and a constant looking to Christ, who is your righteousness (1 Corinthians 1:30).

   c. Feet shod with the preparation of the gospel of peace (verse 15)—eagerness to present the gospel wherever and whenever possible.

   d. The shield of faith (verse 16)—implicit trust in God's Word.

   e. The helmet of salvation (verse 17)—confidence in the hope of salvation and the sufficiency of the cross.

   f. The sword of the Spirit (verse 17)—knowledge of the specific statements of God to apply at the point of temptation.

   g. All kinds of prayers and requests (verse 18)—prayerful attitude of thankfulness and dependence.

Which pieces are you in need of most right now, and how can you apply them to your life?

3. When it comes to resisting Satan, in addition to using Scripture as suggested in the chapter, we must learn to pray against demonic activity in our families, church, and specific individuals. We can do this best by putting on the armor of God daily and rebuking satanic activity through the use of Scripture. In what specific ways can you be praying right now?

CHAPTER 12

Trapped Again

When you are down, get up!

Walter Payton, who played football for the Chicago Bears for 13 seasons as a running back, at one time held the league's record for the most rushing yards. He carried the ball a total of 16,726 yards. As football players go, he was a small man—he was 5 feet 10 inches tall, and weighed 200 pounds.

The total distance Payton carried the ball adds up to more than 9 miles. Now, imagine carrying the ball that distance and being thrown to the ground by someone bigger than you every 4.4 yards—that is, 3801 times. Someone asked him, "How did you do it?" He replied simply, "I just kept getting up!"

By now I hope you have made some progress in tackling that habit that wouldn't budge. Maybe you've gone a day or even a week without slipping back into the same old sin, so you're probably starting to feel optimistic that at last, you can see the light at the end of the tunnel. You can finally begin feeling better about yourself…right?

Wrong! Be careful here, because this is precisely the moment at which most of us find ourselves failing again. We think our past is history, and so we let down our guard. But that is just the invitation Satan is looking for to come barreling back into our lives.

So does that mean we should we conclude that we were deluded—that victory isn't possible after all? Not at all! We should be assured that our victory is most definitely real. But it is not enough to stand up once, only to fall down again.

So what happens to keep us from breaking the cycle for good? Several things, possibly. Jerry G. Dunn, a former alcoholic, discovered a pattern among alcoholics—a pattern that he illuminated in his book *God Is for the Alcoholic.*[7] After reading it, I've concluded that all of us experience this cycle in one form or another. Dunn did a lot of research to find out why alcoholics would quit drinking and enjoy a period of abstinence, only to return to drinking. God gave him insight into this problem, and that's when he noticed the cycle, which Dunn says can take a week, a month, or even years to complete.

First, the alcoholic desires never to take another drink. He's had it. Never again will he make a fool of himself—waking up in strange rooms, not knowing how he got there. Just remembering the humiliation of the past keeps him sober for a while.

Such a feeling is usually the first step toward freedom from any habit. We are tired of gaining weight, losing our temper, or whatever. We become so weary of failure that we begin to seek a way to deliverance. But there are many Christians who haven't reached this point. They are not yet weary of their sin. Or, perhaps they had gotten rid of their more obnoxious habits, but not the subtle ones. Some sinful habits are still too attractive to discard completely. As we've already learned, God wants us to desire victory for reasons other than personal fulfillment. But usually our quest for freedom begins with a healthy disgust for our failures.

Second, Dunn noticed that as time goes by, alcoholics begin to take pride in their sobriety. They'll say, "You know, I haven't had a drink in three weeks." The alcoholic begins to feel better—he might even get his job back and regain the respect of his children. Soon he begins to have a superior attitude as he watches his friends drink. He thinks to himself, *I'd never act that foolishly again, thank God.* Yet it is difficult for him to avoid the constant bombardment of alcohol. Social drinking is considered acceptable, and his friends invite him to join. He is still proud of his abstinence and yet fears that he just might slip back into his former habit. Dunn says this is what we call "a dry drunk."[8] This man has reached the place where he has to fight against taking another drink. He is disgusted with people who drink. He can't stand the smell of liquor. He becomes irritable, and someone's suggestion that he have a drink becomes a personal insult.

But after enduring the struggle for some time, the alcoholic begins to think he has solved the problems that caused his addiction. He is feeling better physically and mentally. Perhaps he has even begun to attend church, so he thinks his spiritual life is in order. He breathes a sigh of relief. At last, everything will be all right.

Finally, when he feels he has mastered the situation—or at last feels he has his problem under control—opportunities to drink become more numerous than ever. One of his associates says, "Aw, you can handle it." Until that point, he has been refusing such offers. But suddenly he feels he is the master of a whole new world. Surely he is able to handle a single drink. So he says yes—just once.

At this point, Dunn says, the alcoholic goes in one of two directions. If he is able to stop at one drink, he confirms his conclusion that he can handle drinking. He loses his fear of alcohol. He finds it easy to take another drink when it is offered. But more often, that one drink re-inflames his passion for alcohol. Dunn writes, "One drink might be enough to plunge him to the very depths of alcoholism as quickly as one can be pushed over a cliff."[9]

Either way, the end result is the same: The alcoholic will become completely victimized by the bottle again. In his book, Dunn mentioned a doctor who took ten years to complete the cycle. By drinking half a glass of beer, he started another binge that eventually ruined his home and cost him his practice.

Your problem may not be alcoholism, but my guess is that your cycle follows the same pattern. I know I've gone through the same steps with other sins. Let's take a look now at what we can learn from such failures.

What Does God Want to Teach Us?

God uses our failures to teach us several lessons. The moment we fail, we receive a crash course in theology. We are vividly reminded that "pride goes before destruction, a haughty spirit before a fall" (Proverbs 16:18). John Bunyan was right when he said, "He that is low need fear no fall."

Remember the Israelites at Ai? They had just conquered Jericho, a city fortified with huge, strong walls. God had done a miracle for the Israelities—the walls had collapsed, and the city became theirs. The next city on their agenda was the smaller town of Ai. Fresh from the victory of Jericho, the men decided that only a small contingent was necessary for conquering Ai. But the Israelites were quickly defeated. Their self-confidence was ill-founded. In their enthusiasm for victory, they had overlooked the sin that was in the camp. Their past victory was no guarantee for future success.

We must learn that our most dangerous moment is when we think we have finally mastered our situation. A series of victories sets us up for a fall. We should never say, "This is one sin I have under control. I'll never commit it again."

God loathes self-righteousness—a superior, judgmental attitude. How easy it is to say, "I'd never do what *he* did!" Anyone who says that has no idea of what he is capable of doing. There is no sin beyond the capacity of any one of us. If we have not succumbed to the same degree of evil as others, it is because we have not had the same opportunities to do evil, and more important, because God's grace has restrained us.

Remember the Pharisee who went into the temple to pray? He's generally remembered for reciting all of his good works to God. But what we often overlook is that he didn't take the credit for his high moral standing. At least he said, "God, I thank *you* that I am not like other people" (Luke 18:11). But even though he *thanked God* that he was not like others, he did not receive God's mercy. Why? Because even good works done in God's name are never the basis for acceptance. The prayer of the humble tax collector was received precisely because he understood that the basis of his acceptance was God's mercy alone.

Even the oft-repeated assertion (usually recited by smug, self-possessed Christians who never seem to struggle like the rest of us) "There but for the grace of God go I" can be said self-righteously. We think that we are different, that we are better than others, because we have attracted God's favor. Even such refined self-righteousness is anathema to God. He wants us to see that, in essence, all human beings are the same. If we are objects of His special grace, it is because of His sovereign pleasure, and not because we are better than others.

Our failures help us to learn these lessons. I don't know what Paul's thorn in the flesh was, but it originated with the devil. He says it was "a messenger of Satan, to torment me," "in order to keep me from becoming conceited" (2 Corinthians 12:7). That weakness was expressly allowed by God to keep Paul from pride and self-righteousness.

God does not cause us to sin, but He uses our sins to remind us of our weakness. We are less tempted to judge others, and more understanding of their failures, when we become well acquainted with the wickedness of our own heart. We then learn how to view others with humility, considering ourselves, lest we also be tempted (Galatians 6:1). When we are caught by sin, God uses the experience to teach us about His righteousness and His hatred of sin.

God also wants us to appreciate the wonder of His grace. "Where sin increased, grace increased all the more" (Romans 5:20). Because of pride, I find it hard to admit that I need God's grace so continually, so desperately. How we would all like to be able to say, "I've not committed that sin in ten years." But our continual problems with sin press us toward the cross. Again and again we are confronted with Calvary; we are forced to come with nothing in our hands so we can receive God's provision freely given from His grace.

Peter summarizes it all for us by saying, "Clothe yourselves with humility toward one another, because 'God opposes the proud, but shows favor to the humble.' Humble yourselves, therefore, under God's mighty hand, that he may lift you up in due time" (1 Peter 5:5-6).

Signposts to Failure

At Niagara Falls, there is a point of no return in the river—a place where the water rushes so fiercely that it would be impossible to make progress against the stream. At that point, going over the falls is inevitable. There are warning signs that tell the unwary where that point is, but some foolhardy souls either have ignored the signs or not seen them. Most who went past that point are not around to tell us which it was.

We have our warning signs too. Generally, they're slow leaks and not blowouts that stop us. Failure, actually, is quite predictable. We can tell whether we are on our way to the point of no return.

What are those signposts? The first is a feeling of self-satisfaction, a sigh of relief that finally we have everything under control. At that moment, we are vulnerable because our confidence rests with ourselves and our past record rather than with the Lord. Remember the alcoholic? He thinks he has drinking under control. Yet he must be reminded that he never has drinking under control. Even at Alcoholics Anonymous meetings the participants are trained to say, "I am an alcoholic." And they must remember that fact even after they have been dry for ten years.

Friend, we are sinners. And we will continue to be until the day we die. We must beware of thinking that we have any sin permanently under control. "So, if you think you are standing firm, be careful that you don't fall!" (1 Corinthians 10:12).

Then there is the danger of making a hidden provision for defeat. Dave wanted desperately to overcome his addiction to pornography, but he kept some inappropriate DVDs in his room just in case he was tempted. Or consider the woman who wants to stop smoking but keeps a pack of cigarettes in the drawer, thinking that eventually she might need them.

Our mind is like a huge house with many rooms. We might be willing to clean up the kitchen, the living room, and even some of the bedrooms. But what about the closet crammed with junk? Perhaps it is precious to us, for it represents one small part of our life we are not willing to surrender to the searchlight of the Holy Spirit. But Christ wants to be the master of our entire life. He wants to reveal everything that is hidden. There is only one way we can meet God's requirement, and that is by refusing to hold tightly onto any room in our life that can be used as a retreat from our spiritual commitment.

God wants us to perform radical surgery on sinful habits. We must burn all our bridges. This is what Jesus taught in the Sermon on the Mount. Immediately following His remark about the sin of lust, He made a shocking statement:

> If your right eye causes you to stumble, gouge it out and throw it away. It is better for you to lose one part of your body than for your whole body to be thrown into hell. And if your right hand causes you to stumble, cut it off and throw it away. It is better for you to lose one part of your body than for your whole body to go into hell (Matthew 5:29-30).

Once an eye is gouged out or a hand cut off, there is no chance of it being put back. The separation is final; there is no hidden agenda for a comeback. Paul wrote, "Clothe yourselves with the Lord Jesus Christ, and do not think about how to gratify the desires of the flesh" (Romans 13:14).

There is also a signpost for spiritual coasting. That's what happens when we begin to crowd God and His Word to the circumference of our lives. This happens so subtly as we feel pressured to keep up with the responsibilities of life: jobs, spouses, children, hobbies, church, friends—even TV, the Internet, the newest cell phone...

I was once on a boat that left the shore so quietly that I scarcely noticed it. That's the way most backsliding happens—slowly and without fanfare. Not until we experience tragic failure do we realize how far we have drifted from the shore. God prefers that we be either cold or hot, not lukewarm (Revelation 3:16). The reason is simple:

Someone who is cold seeks fire, whereas someone who is lukewarm is generally comfortable and sees no need for change. He is so self-satisfied that he doesn't know how bad off he is! The believers at the city of Laodicea, to whom these words were directed, were lukewarm. They had drifted from their love for Christ, and hadn't even noticed it. Gardeners tell us that weeds will always take over when we stop growing healthy plants and pulling weeds out by their roots.

Finally, there is a signpost for compromise. That's when we tolerate personal sin for just a little while. I have seen a man shatter a cement wall with a huge hammer. The first time he hit it, the wall was as solid as ever. Even after twenty blows the wall seemed immovable. But he kept at it. After a while, the wall began to crumble a bit, though it still stood firm and upright. But it was weakening! First one small piece fell, then another, then gradually the wall collapsed.

That's the way sin is. It is true that we can tolerate sin without having it ruin us—but we can't do that for long. Compromise might sometimes be possible without disastrous results, but eventually it weakens our resistance. How many Christian leaders have we heard of recently who have become involved in the sin of adultery? Most such affairs probably began innocently enough—first they were just friends. But then the mind was allowed to entertain a few fantasies and some lustful thoughts. Such escapades of the imagination will eventually weaken a person's resistance. Like the cement wall, people—even pastors—can remain solid for a while, believing all is well. But in time, they will collapse.

Watch for these signposts. They are warnings for you on your journey. When you see them, get back on course and keep your eyes on Jesus, "the author and finisher of our faith" (Hebrews 12:2 KJV).

How Long Before You Stand Again?

You've been caught in the old trap; you're back in the same rut. How long should you stay there? Satan would like to say, "Forever. After all, what's the use? Since you're not really sure you'll be victorious next time, why bother?"

You could be tempted to agree. Human nature resents the idea that we must come back to God without an "award for special merit" sign pinned on our vest. We are uncomfortable accepting mercy that we don't deserve. We hesitate to come back immediately without a period of probation. We may even want to appease our guilt by punishing ourselves by withdrawing from God and His people. So we postpone our appointment with the Almighty until we have proven we mean business and that we will never fall again. Furthermore, we argue, guilt is good for us. It will teach us never to do that again!

God thinks otherwise. To think we must straighten up before we come back to Him reveals a misunderstanding of the cross. We are to come solely on the merit of the blood of Christ, not on the merit of our own efforts. *Guilt is not God pushing us away from Him; it is God trying to put His arms around us.*

So is guilt good for us? Yes, when it teaches us how uncomfortable the aftereffects of sin can be. But guilt alone shouldn't be our motivation for changing our behavior. At any rate, nowhere in the Bible do we read that God uses guilt itself to discipline His children. The natural consequences of sin will do that, for they teach us how reprehensible sin can be. But guilt is not God's means of discipline; it is contrary to the cross. God's method of motivating us to live righteously is His love and grace.

Consider what Paul wrote: "I urge you, brothers and sisters, in view of God's mercy, to offer your bodies as a living sacrifice, holy and pleasing to God—this is your true and proper worship" (Romans 12:1). Grace, freely given, does not provide us license to sin. Rather, it should motivate us to give ourselves without reservation to the One who loves us so freely, so deeply. Whenever you sin, God wants you to come back into fellowship immediately. Learn your lessons, but within His forgiveness—not outside of it.

You may have heard that it is good to keep "short accounts" with God. Don't let sin pile up in your life. Don't think that you have to wait until the church doors open, or even until the end of the day, before taking care of your sin. Confess it the moment it comes to your attention. In fact, don't keep short accounts with God; keep *current* accounts with God. Whether you are driving your car, working in the office, or doing chores at home, you can be engaging in dialogue with God. As you speak to Him, He replies through His Word.

Listen to the hope of the Scriptures for all who sin:

> This is what the LORD says: "When people fall down, do they not get up? When someone turns away, do they not return?" (Jeremiah 8:4).

> The LORD upholds all who fall and lifts up all who are bowed down (Psalm 145:14).

> Do not gloat over me, my enemy! Though I have fallen, I will rise. Though I sit in darkness, the LORD will be my light (Micah 7:8).

> Though the righteous fall seven times, they rise again, but the wicked stumble when calamity strikes (Proverbs 24:16).

> The LORD makes firm the steps of the one who delights in him; though he may stumble, he will not fall, for the LORD upholds him with his hand (Psalm 37:23-24).

You *can* say no to that stubborn habit by saying yes to God once again!

ACTION STEP: After reading this chapter, do you get a sense for just how eager God is to help His children when they stumble? Make a conscious effort—daily—to remind yourself that God's grace really is greater than your sin. He still loves you even when you fall. When sin gets you down, don't let it keep you down. Confess your wrong-doing, and get up!

Questions for Personal Reflection or Group Study

1. Think back to the last time you were trapped by your weakness. Did you have any indication that you were going to give in to the temptation? What can you learn from that experience?

2. In what ways do we sometimes entertain temptation, thinking that we can handle it and know when to stop? What does this type of attitude reveal about us?

3. What do you think might be the best antidote to drifting in your spiritual life? Or is there more than one precaution that is needed? Think of ways that you can lessen the chances of stumbling spiritually. Write them down.

4. Why do we often delay our confession of sin after we have sinned? What lessons have we not yet learned?

5. Why do you think sin is so subtle? Spend some time in prayer right now. Ask God to bring to light the areas of your life that need renewal, and thank Him that He has given you that possibility through His Son Jesus.

Writing the Last Chapter

You have now read and pondered the basic principles that God can use to renew your mind and change your behavior. Where do you go from here? What can you do to follow through on any commitment you have made?

This book is incomplete unless it is applied; we must not only know the truth, but do it. For this reason, you will write the last chapter. Most of us do not need more truth than we already have; what we need is to weave what we know into the fabric of our daily lives. So here is your opportunity to take over where this book leaves off. You will decide how this book will end with regard to the way you deal with temptation.

To write the last chapter, purchase a thick notebook. It will belong to you alone—no editor will read its contents to see if it is marketable. There is no need to review your grammar or use a dictionary to check your spelling. This chapter is between you and God.

This notebook will become your spiritual journal, a chronicle of where you are in your life, where you want to be, and the steps you will take to get there. Of course, you can write whatever you wish in your book. But in the questions below, I am including some suggestions that you may want to incorporate into your journal.

Questions for Your Personal Notebook

1. Write a letter to God, telling Him about your past—the failures and the successes. Be sure to include mention of your weaknesses or bad habits. Share with God the desires of your heart. Specifically, tell Him what you would like to have Him do in your life during the next month, the next six months, and the next year. As you do this, concentrate on your character qualities, remembering that God's goal is that you be conformed to the image of His Son (Romans 8:29).

2. Write out special prayer requests for others: your wife or husband, your children, your relatives, your friends. Be specific.

3. Ask God to give you wisdom as you outline a strategy for becoming the person you believe He wants you to be. This will include items such as beginning each day with God, memorizing two or more verses of Scripture a week, learning and engaging in the ministry of intercession for others.

4. Try to anticipate the ways that Satan and the flesh will attempt to prevent you from following through with your commitment, such as sleeping too late, watching TV, being disorganized. Minimize the possibility that you will fail. How much is a disciplined relationship with God worth to you?

5. Record in your notebook, on a regular basis, things such as:

- specific prayer requests and their answers;
- special observations you make about the Scriptures that are of particular help, and
- the lessons that God teaches you.

Let your notebook become a monument to God's faithfulness in your life. If you do, the most important chapter in this book will be the last one, the one that you are writing. The apostle Paul acknowledged that the best book is a life lived in the power of the Spirit: "You yourselves are our letter, written on our hearts, known and read by everyone" (2 Corinthians 3:2). May God help you to begin today.

Tips for Small Group Discussion

After going through each chapter on your own, take some time to go back over the material and go a little deeper. Here are a few thoughts on how to make the most of your time as you prepare to get together with others who are going through this book as a group.

Set ground rules. You don't need many. Here are two:

First, you'll want to commit, as a group, to see this through to completion. Significant personal growth happens when group members spend enough time together to really get to know each other. It doesn't have to be every week, but you do need to establish some element of consistency to your time together. If you are working through this book on your own, make a commitment to yourself to finish.

Second, agree together that everyone's story is important. Time is probably the most valuable commodity today, so if you have just an hour to spend together, do your best to give each person ample time to express concerns, pass along insights, and be a participating member of the group. Small-group discussions aren't monologues; however, a one-person-dominated discussion isn't always a bad thing either. Not only is your role in a small group to explore and expand your own understanding, it's also to support one another. If one group member truly needs the floor for a more extended period, give it to that person. At times the needs of one outweigh the needs of many. Use good judgment and allow extra space when needed; *your* time might be the next occasion your group meets.

Meet regularly. Choose a time and place and stick to it. Don't be surprised if this becomes a struggle. Go into this study with that expectation and push through it. If you are working through this book on your own, set aside a weekly time and place where you know you will be able to concentrate.

Let God lead. Each time you get together, guess who else is in the room? That's right—God. Be sensitive to how He is leading. Does your time need to be structured? Then following the book's structure is a good idea. Does the time need breathing room instead? Then take a breath, step back, and see what God does.

Talk openly. You'll all be a little tentative at first. It's okay if someone is a little hesitant to unpack all his or her struggles in front of friends or new acquaintances. Maybe that person is just a little skeptical about the value of revealing the deepest things of the heart with others. Maybe some are afraid of what their revelations might sound or look like. Getting people to the point of being uncomfortable isn't the goal; rather, the goal is a safe place to share and be. In all that, don't neglect the most important goal: helping others with their struggles and to find meaning for their lives.

And don't forget that God has brought all of you together. No one is a part of this group by random chance. Give people a chance to stretch themselves. Let them dip their feet in the water of honest discussion. Help them find healing.

If you're going through this book on your own, even being honest with yourself can be difficult. Because you're not able to talk openly with others, take time to record all your thoughts and emotions, and let God do His work.

Stay on task. If structure isn't your group's strength, then try this approach: Spend a few minutes sharing general comments about the study, and then go through each study question and give everyone in the group a chance to respond to it. While you're listening to others, write down thoughts that their words prompt within you. And during your times of prayer, listen to each other's prayers so that all of you can genuinely support one another through prayer.

If you're working through this book on your own, make sure that your study time is free of distractions. Don't work in front of the TV or while you're waiting for the bus. Honor the changes God wants to make in your life by taking this book seriously through focused study.

Follow-up. Don't let the life applications in this book drift away without further action. Be accountable to each other and refer back to thoughts from previous chapters often. Take time at the beginning of each meeting to review past principles and see how you're doing. Be sure to pray for each other in between your meetings. If God brings certain group members to mind during the course of a given day, take a moment to call or email that person just to encourage him and ask, "How are you doing?"

If you're working through this book on your own, don't just keep plowing forward from one chapter to the next. Take time to review whether you are making progress. Have you been applying what you've learned? Reach down deep and be honest with God and yourself. It's your best chance at spiritual growth.

Bibliography

Adams, Jay E. *Competent to Counsel.* Grand Rapids: Baker Book House, 1970.

———. *You Can Sweeten a Sour Marriage.* Grand Rapids: Baker Book House, 1975.

Augustine. *Confessions.* Oxford: Clarendon Press, 1992.

Bubeck, Mark. *The Adversary: The Christian Versus Demonic Activity.* Chicago: Moody Press, 1975.

Christenson, Larry. *The Renewed Mind.* Minneapolis: Bethany Fellowship, 1974.

Christians Unite. "Two Great Lies by James Stalker." Articles, http://articles.christians unite.com/article9614.shtml (accessed August 2, 2007).

Dunn, Jerry G. *God Is for the Alcoholic.* Chicago: Moody Press, 1986.

Kiev, Ari. *A Strategy for Daily Living.* New York: Free Press, 1973.

Shelhamer, E.E. "Traits of the Self-Life." Harrisburg, VA: Christian Light Publications, 1994.

Spiegelberg, Nancy. "If Only I Had Known You." Godthoughts, http://www.god thoughts.com/only.htm (accessed August 2, 2007).

Meyer, F.B., quoted in Guido, Michael. "The Book of Acts: Message Three." Guido Gardens Online, http://www.the-sower.org/acts/03.htm (accessed August 2, 2007).

Notes

1. Delavan Leonard Pierson, *The Northfield Year-Book for Each New Day* (Chicago: Fleming H. Revell, 1896), p. 211.

2. John Newton, "Amazing Grace," published in 1779.

3. Nancy Spiegelberg, "If Only I Had Known You," © 1974 at http://www.god thoughts.com/only.htm.

4. *Traits of the Self-Life* (Chicago: Good News Publishers, n.d.).

5. Ari Kiev, *A Strategy for Daily Living* (Backinprint.com, 2008), p. 3.

6. Lewis Sperry Chafer and John F. Walvoord, *Major Bible Themes,* rev. ed. (Grand Rapids: Zondervan, 1974), p. 74.

7. Jerry Dunn, *God Is for the Alcoholic* (Chicago: Moody, 1986).

8. Dunn, *God Is for the Alcoholic*, p. 64.

9. Dunn, *God Is for the Alcoholic*, p. 67.

Other Harvest House Books
by Erwin W. Lutzer

Life-Changing Bible Verses
You Should Know
(with Rebecca Lutzer)

Do you desire to experience the life-changing power of God's Word? Do you long to hide God's Word in your heart, but don't know where to start?

In this book, Bible teacher Erwin Lutzer and his wife, Rebecca, have carefully selected more than 100 Bible verses that speak directly to the most important issues of life, and explained the very practical ways those verses can encourage and strengthen you.

The Power of a Clear Conscience

Do you struggle with feelings of guilt about your past? Are you bogged down by a conscience that haunts or imprisons you?

This is not how God intends for you to live. Your conscience was not created to hold you prisoner, but to guide you and point you to freedom from guilt and bad habits.

Learn how to live in the power of a clear conscience by replacing guilt with joy, exchanging your hurts for healing, and realizing the extent of God's forgiveness and love for you.

No life is beyond God's power to bring about change!

Covering Your Life in Prayer

Every Christian longs for a better and more intimate prayer life. And one of the most effective ways you can grow more powerful in prayer is to learn from the prayers of others. In this book you'll discover new ways to pray—new requests, concerns, and thanksgivings you can bring to God's throne of grace. A wonderful resource for expanding your prayer horizons and enriching your relationship with God.

The Cross in the Shadow of the Crescent

Islam is on the rise all over the West, including in America. In this compelling book, Erwin Lutzer urges Christians to see this as both an opportunity to share the gospel and a reason for concern. Along the way, you'll find helpful answers to these questions and more:

- How does Islam's growing influence affect me personally?
- In what ways are our freedoms of speech and religion in danger?
- How can I extend Christ's love to Muslims around me?

A sensitive, responsible, and highly informative must-read!

To learn more about Harvest House books and
to read sample chapters, visit our website:

www.harvesthousepublishers.com

HARVEST HOUSE PUBLISHERS
EUGENE, OREGON